D1095630

Twayne's English Authors Series

Sylvia E. Bowman, *Editor*

INDIANA UNIVERSITY

Sir William Temple

(TEAS) 109

Sir William Temple

By ROBERT C. STEENSMA

University of Utah

Twayne Publishers, Inc.   ::   New York

For SHARON

Preface

In the year 1700 many Englishmen would have remembered Sir William Temple as the man who had negotiated the Triple Alliance and the Treaty of Nimeguen, conducted the negotiations which brought about the marriage of William of Orange to Mary Stuart, proposed a workable and much-needed revision of the Privy Council, sat as a member of Parliament, thrice declined appointment as secretary of state, and published a number of highly readable essays on topics ranging from politics and gardening to literature and ethics. Although an occasional enemy such as Bishop Burnet might write harsh words about him, Temple's reputation seemed secure.

But literary history has a way of tarnishing bright reputations, and such has been the case with Temple's. Although his collected works were reprinted eight times between 1720 and 1814, there is still no standard edition of his writings; and, except for two fine book-length studies by Clara Marburg and Homer E. Woodbridge, there is a dearth of critical and scholarly commentary about him and his work. The articles which have thus far appeared deal generally with his relationship to Swift or with other narrowly circumscribed aspects of his career; and the critical comments in literary histories have been, for the most part, condescending or glib. Temple is remembered today by students of literature as the dilettante essayist and scholar whose comments in *An Essay upon the Ancient and Modern Learning* brought the quarrel between the ancients and moderns from France to England and stimulated young Jonathan Swift to write *The Battle of the Books* and *A Tale of a Tub*.

The purpose of this book is to survey all of Temple's writings from his early essays and romances to those mature works written in the retirement and serenity of Sheen and Moor Park, several of which were published posthumously. Generally these works will be discussed topically and, wherever possible, chronologically. After Chapter 1, the details of Temple's life and political career enter into my discussion only where necessary to illuminate his thought. Finally, there will be a chapter on Temple's personal and intellectual relationship to Swift and another on his literary reputation since 1700. Because of the general unavailability of most of Temple's works, I have taken the liberty to quote copiously from his writings.

During the course of writing this book I have called upon the assistance of a number of people who have been generous in their willingness to help, among whom are Sylvia E. Bowman, general editor-in-chief of the Twayne English Authors Series; the late King Hendricks, former head of the Department of English at Utah State University; and Diane Elwood Hall, a typist of patience, skill, and, at times, intuition.

Perhaps my greatest debts are to Arthur L. Cooke of the University of Kentucky, in whose doctoral seminar I was first introduced to the writings of Temple, and to my wife, Sharon Carol Steensma, whose good-natured acceptance of the role of a scholar's wife made the writing of this book much more enjoyable.

ROBERT C. STEENSMA

University of Utah

Contents

Contents

Chronology

1628	William Temple born April 25 in London; eldest child of Sir John Temple and Mary Hammond Temple.
1628–1638	Spent boyhood in London with occasional visits to Ireland with father on business.
1638–1639(?)	Mother died on September 5, 1638; young Temple sent to live with his uncle, Dr. Henry Hammond, the famous divine, at Penshurst.
1639(?)–1643	Attended school at Bishop Stortford School near London.
1644–1647(?)	Entered Emmanuel College, Cambridge, as a fellow commoner; tutored by Ralph Cudworth, the Cambridge Platonist; left college without his degree.
1648–1650	Set out on a journey to the Continent; met Dorothy Osborne on the Isle of Wight; traveled in France.
1651–1652	Second trip to the Continent, probably visiting Holland, Germany, and Flanders; composed the early essays and romances.
1652–1654	Carried on extensive correspondence with Dorothy Osborne, to whom he probably became engaged in February, 1652. After family opposition, the couple was married on Christmas Day, 1654.
1655	First son, John, born at Reading on December 18.
1656	Moved to Ireland and remained there until 1663 or 1664, living in Dublin and County Carlow.
1661	Elected to Irish Parliament from County Carlow. In July or August, went to England as a member of a delegation to King Charles, returning in late 1662.
1663(?)–1664(?)	Returned to London with family.
1665	Bought house at Sheen in spring or early summer. In July, sent to Coesvelt as intermediary to Bishop of Munster. Appointed to residency at Brussels in early October.
1666	Promoted to baronetcy in January.

1666–1667	Returned to Munster in April to try to prevent Bishop of Munster from breaking treaty.
1667	Met John DeWitt, Grand Pensionary of Holland, at The Hague; returned to London in December.
1668	Proceeded to The Hague in January to negotiate a defensive treaty with the Dutch against Louis XIV; treaty signed in January. Sweden entered the agreement in May to form the Triple Alliance. Appointed ambassador to The Hague in August, 1668; shortly thereafter met William, Prince of Orange.
1670	On June 1, King Charles II signed secret Treaty of Dover with Louis, thus destroying the Triple Alliance. Temple returned to London in September.
1671	Temple's embassy concluded; returned to England with his family.
1671–1674	Retired to Sheen to engage in writing and gardening.
1672	*Observations upon the United Provinces of the Netherlands* published in London.
1673	*An Essay upon the Advancement of Trade in Ireland* published in Dublin. In late October, Temple tried to persuade the ministry to return to policy of the Triple Alliance in his paper *Upon the Conjuncture of Affairs in October 1673.*
1674	Sent to Holland in February to conduct peace negotiations. Shortly thereafter offered post as ambassador-extraordinary to Spain, but declined. In May, appointed ambassador-extraordinary to Holland; arrived at The Hague in July.
1675	Appointed ambassador to the Congress of Nimeguen.
1676–1677	At Nimeguen from July, 1676 to July, 1677. Arranged marriage of William of Orange to Mary Stuart which occurred in November, 1677. Sir John Temple died in November, 1677, his post as master of the rolls in Ireland reverting to Sir William. Offered post as secretary of state to succeed Henry Coventry, but Coventry decided not to resign.
1678	Began third embassy at The Hague in July; visited Nimeguen in August.
1679	Again offered position as secretary of state in January;

declined on grounds of ill health. Death of daughter Diana at age fourteen. Went to Nimeguen for conclusion of congress. Proposed new arrangement of Privy Council to Charles. Elected to House of Commons from Cambridge. *Miscellanea, the First Part,* published at London.

1681 Temple's name stricken from Privy Council list on January 24. Retired to Sheen.

1681– In retirement at Sheen. September 1685, marriage of
1686   son John to Mlle DuPlessis Rambouillet of Paris.

1686   Bought Moor Park in Surrey for two thousand pounds and turned house and property at Sheen over to John; moved to Moor Park in November.

1686– In retirement amid gardens and books at Moor Park.
1699

1689   John died a suicide, for reasons not clear, on April 19. Shortly thereafter Jonathan Swift entered the Temple household.

1690   *Miscellanea, the Second Part,* published at London.

1691   *Memoirs of What Past in Christendom, from the War Begun 1672 to the Peace Concluded 1679 (Memoirs, Part II)* published at London.

1693   Temple suffered severe illness near the end of the year.

1695   Lady Temple died in early February and was buried in Westminster Abbey beside daughter Diana. *An Introduction to the History of England* published in London.

1696   Resigned as master of the rolls, having filled the position by deputy for nearly twenty years.

1698   Drew up codicil to will, leaving one hundred pounds to Swift.

1699   Died on January 27. Interred in Westminster Abbey beside wife and daughter. Heart buried beneath sundial at Moor Park.

1700– Swift, as literary executor, edited and published *Letters*
1709   *Written by Sir William Temple, and Other Ministers of State* (2 volumes, 1700), *Miscellanea, the Third Part* (1701), *Letters to the King, the Prince of Orange, Etc.* (1703), and *Memoirs, the Third Part* (1709), all at London.

CHAPTER 1

Temple and His Times

S IR WILLIAM TEMPLE'S *Essay upon the Ancient and Modern Learning* ends with a quotation which clearly summarizes his philosophy of life: *"That among so many things as are by Men possessed or pursued in the Course of their Lives, all the rest are Bawbles, besides Old Wood to Burn, Old Wine to Drink, Old Friends to Converse with, and Old Books to Read."* [1] When he wrote this passage, probably in the years 1688–90, Temple had been retired for almost a decade to the security of his gardens and his library. Having weathered the uncertain storms of diplomacy, having seen the hard-won fruits of his diplomatic work wasted by a faithless king and his counselors, and having lost his only two children who had lived beyond infancy, Temple could indeed believe that pleasure, in moderation to be sure, was man's greatest happiness. Thus, approaching the last decade of his life, he could say in the essay *Of Heroic Virtue* (1690), "When all is done, Human Life is, at the greatest, and the best but like a froward Child, that must be play'd with and humour'd a little to keep it quiet till it falls asleep, and then the Care is over" (I, 249).

Since his death in 1699 Temple has remained on the periphery of English literary history. Highly praised for his style by some critics, and by others admired for the quiet morality of his life amid the raucous lasciviousness usually associated in the popular mind with the Restoration, Temple has been thought of as dull, hopelessly naïve, and almost ignorant. Representative of all too many moderns' opinions is a recent comment: "these essays make perfect bedtime reading: start one, and almost instantly the mouth opens and the eyes shut." [2] Similarly, George Saintsbury believed that Temple's works are characterized by "the enormity of their ignorance, the complacency of their dogmatism, and the blandness of their superficiality." [3]

On the other hand, the man who knew Temple best—Jonathan

Swift—could not praise him highly enough. Early in his tenure at
Moor Park he could say that "I never read his writings but I prefer him to all others at present in England," and later he asserted
that Temple was the most accomplished writer of his time.[4]
Somewhere between these two extremes perhaps lies the truth.

I *The Man*

Born in 1628, Temple was descended from a prominent and
illustrious family. His grandfather and namesake was William
Temple (1555–1627), a close friend of Sir Philip Sidney, who, ac-
cording to tradition, died in his arms at Zutphen; previously,
Temple had dedicated his edition of the *Dialectics* of Ramus to
Sidney. His father, Sir John Temple, was in the personal service of
Charles I as master of the rolls in Ireland. His mother was Mary
Hammond, daughter of Sir John Hammond, who had been physi-
cian to James I, and the sister of Dr. Henry Hammond, one of the
most learned divines of the early seventeenth century.

We know little about Temple's childhood before the death of
his mother in 1638, when he was sent to live with his uncle, Dr.
Hammond, while his father returned to court. Perhaps a year later
he was sent to the Bishop Stortford School in Hertfordshire, some
thirty miles north of London, where he remained until his fifteenth birthday. On August 31, 1644, he entered Emmanuel College, Cambridge, as a fellow commoner. Again, except for the
comments of his sister, Martha (later Lady Giffard), we have
little evidence concerning Temple's stay at Cambridge. His tutor
was the famous Cambridge Platonist, Ralph Cudworth; but
Temple benefited little from his master's influence. As Lady
Giffard tells us in her sketch of her brother, Cudworth "would
have engaged him in the harsh studies of logick and phylosophy
wch his humor was too lively to pursue," for he was more interested in tennis than in learning.[5] At any rate, he left the university without taking his degree, perhaps in 1647, to travel abroad.

His departure from the university marked the beginning of his
contact with the larger world of politics and letters in which he
was to be active for the remainder of his life. Although his movements between 1648 and 1652 are hard to trace, Lady Giffard tells
us that he spent two years in France and learned to speak French
perfectly.[6] He returned to England in 1650, but shortly thereafter

made a second trip abroad to visit Holland, Germany, and Flanders over a two-year period.

Probably the most important result of his first travels abroad was his first meeting with the beautiful, talented Dorothy Osborne on the Isle of Wight, where the ill-fated Charles I was being held prisoner. Temple perhaps began corresponding with her before 1652, but no letters from either party previous to this year are extant. Dorothy's letters, beginning in December, 1652, have been preserved, though they were not made known to the public until Courtenay published extracts from them in 1836. From December, 1652, to October, 1654, we have now published seventy-seven letters from Dorothy to Temple, most of them undated; but his letters to her, with one exception, have been lost. Her light and witty letters tell us much about Temple's activities during these years.

Beset as their courtship was by family disagreements and by her illness, they were married on Christmas Day, 1654; and, after a honeymoon at Sir Richard Franklin's estate in Hertfordshire, they moved to London. Their first child, John, was born a year after the wedding, and in 1656 the young family moved to Ireland. Between 1656 and 1663 Temple and his wife divided their time between Sir John's house in Dublin and a country place which William built on his father's estate in County Carlow. The years in Ireland were not happy ones; Lady Giffard says that the young couple lost five children during this period.[7]

Nevertheless, the residence in Ireland proved happier in terms of Temple's career. In February, 1660, he was elected to the Irish Parliament from Carlow, and he was returned in 1661. During the second session he served on one committee which sought means of advancing Irish trade, and on another which drafted modifications to the Act of Settlement to safeguard the interests of the Irish Protestants by confirming Cromwell's settlement of land titles. In the summer of 1661 Temple traveled to London as a member of a delegation which sought to persuade the king to pass the amended act, and it was then that he met Charles II for the first time.

In May, 1663, the Irish Parliament was prorogued; the Temples soon returned to London; and by 1665 the family was established at Sheen in Surrey. At this time, King Charles II asked Temple to represent him on a diplomatic mission to the Bishop of Munster in order to negotiate a treaty by which the Bishop, in return for a sizable English subsidy, was to invade the United Provinces with a force of twenty thousand men. Temple was also to make certain that the Bishop carried out his agreement. Although the plague had been raging in London since November of the previous year, and although Temple was understandably reluctant about leaving Dorothy, who was again pregnant, he accepted, went to Munster, negotiated the treaty in a few days in July, and quickly returned to England.

The mission to Munster must have whetted Temple's taste for diplomacy, for he twice suggested to his friend Arlington that he be appointed to the residency in Brussels, a position which was granted to him in October; and, by November 19, he was holding his first audience with the Spanish viceroy. His duties at Brussels consisted of making observations and reports, watching to see that the Spanish maintained their neutrality, and cultivating the friendship of the local officials. In the meantime, the Bishop of Munster having shown signs of reneging on his treaty, Temple was sent to talk with him, only to find that the Bishop had already signed a treaty with the Dutch at Cleves.

In January, 1666, Arlington notified Temple of his promotion to the baronetcy—the only reward he was ever to receive for his public service. For the most part, he himself had had to bear the heavy expenses of his diplomatic work, for which his private fortune was as yet inadequate. Not until his father's death in November, 1677, were his finances sufficient to permit him to live without rigid economy. A baronetcy must have seemed a rather hollow honor when the government owed him several hundred pounds and when his creditors were becoming anxious.

Temple was back in London during the latter part of 1667, and at the beginning of the new year he received instructions to proceed to The Hague to discuss with his friend John DeWitt the possibility of an Anglo-Dutch alliance to protect Spain from the ambitions of France. The proposed treaty was rapidly negotiated; it was signed by the English and the Dutch on January 23, 1668, and by the Swedes on May 5. Thus, the Triple Alliance against King Louis of France was forged. Returning to London on June 22, Temple was received warmly by the king and his court.

A reward in the form of the ambassadorship to The Hague was

soon offered him; he at first hesitated but then accepted it upon the advice of his father. He arrived at Rotterdam during the latter part of August, 1668. The ostensible purpose of his mission was to strengthen the Triple Alliance and to implement its provisions; more specifically, he was to supervise the payment of Spanish subsidies to Sweden in fulfillment of the Treaty of Aix (1668), to seek revision of the Anglo-Dutch maritime treaty so as to solve the problem of the rivalry between the two East India companies, and to alleviate the difficulties of English settlers in Dutch-held Surinam. Stifled by diplomatic protocol, Temple found himself frustrated in pursuing trivial and unjust commercial claims. The Spanish matter was resolved in less than a year, but the problems with the Dutch were not settled so expeditiously.

Thus Temple's first embassy was largely a failure. He had soon realized that the British ministry, never intending to honor the Triple Alliance, was seeking an opportunity to break it. Charles, having been converted to Catholicism and secretly seeking to restore England to the spiritual dominion of Rome, allied himself with King Louis in the secret Treaty of Dover, negotiated by Arlington and Colbert on June 1, 1670, in which Charles agreed to join Louis in his war against the Dutch and to restore Catholicism to England—for which Charles was to receive five million francs. Determined to prevent the repudiation of the Triple Alliance, Temple returned to London in September, but ten months of ceaseless effort failed to save the coalition. Disgusted and heartsick, he concluded his embassy at The Hague, returned his family to England, and retired to Sheen.

Nevertheless, his thoughts were never far from foreign affairs in the seclusion of his garden and library.[8] Temple felt that England, for her own safety as well as honor, must return to the Triple Alliance by concluding a separate peace with Holland. Perhaps this belief motivated him to return to the king's service as envoy to The Hague in February, 1674. Later in the same month he declined, upon the advice of his father, the post of ambassador extraordinary to Spain in place of Sir William Godolphin; but in April, he was appointed ambassador extraordinary to The Hague and arrived there the next month.

In March, 1675, he was nominated ambassador to the Congress of Nimeguen, where he remained until July, 1677. At the congress, he sought to bring about a peace which would protect England

and Holland from French aggression. But his efforts were frustrated: the treaty, signed in 1679, did not permanently check Louis XIV; and the French were permitted to retain possession of the Franche Comte (Free Countship of Burgundy) and of certain areas in Flanders.

Temple's last major accomplishment in public affairs was perhaps his greatest and most influential: the negotiation of marriage of Prince William of Orange, his close friend, to Mary Stuart, daughter of the Duke of York. The Prince first approached him about the matter in April, 1676. Two or three days later Prince William brought his letters for the Duke and King Charles to Lady Temple, who carried them to England. He was invited to visit England in September, 1677; and, after the customary negotiations, in which Temple played a major role, the wedding took place in November.

During these years Temple was twice offered the position of secretary of state. In June, 1677, his son John arrived at Nimeguen with a letter from Danby informing him that Charles wanted him to return to England to succeed Henry Coventry as secretary of state. Temple declined, probably because of his reluctance and inability to pay the ten thousand pounds asked by Coventry. Although Charles later expressed his willingness to supply the money himself, the matter was dropped when Coventry decided not to resign. When the offer was repeated in January, 1679, Temple's ill health caused him to decline the office again. Tragedy struck the Temples in March, 1679, when their only daughter, Diane, died of smallpox at the age of fourteen. Of their nine children, only John now survived; but he, too, would bring sorrow to the family within a decade.

At this same time, during the unsettled days following the Popish Plot, Temple devised a council scheme intended to develop a closer relationship between king and Parliament and to frustrate the designs of the Earl of Shaftesbury and the Duke of Monmouth. He proposed the formation of a new privy council consisting of fifteen of the wealthiest and most influential lords and commoners. After Charles's approval, the plan was put into operation; but the indifference of Commons and the machinations of Shaftesbury and Monmouth brought it into disrepute and consequent failure.

Disgusted with Charles's duplicity and discouraged by his own failure to reconcile the factions that were dividing the English nation in foreign and domestic matters, Temple withdrew from public affairs in the early part of 1681. Shortly thereafter he learned that he had fallen into disfavor with Charles and that his name had been removed from the list of the king's councillors. He now once again retired to the seclusion of Sheen, never again to take an active part in public affairs.

Sometime in 1686, Temple, who had been financially independent since the death of his father nine years earlier, divided his estate with his son, gave him possession of the house and grounds at Sheen, and purchased a place in Surrey for two thousand pounds. He renamed the new estate Moor Park, probably in pleasant memory of his visits to the home of Sir Richard Franklin, and moved there in November.

When the Revolution of 1688 came, James II fled from the country; and Prince William of Orange, Temple's friend of long standing, landed in England to be crowned with his wife Mary. Although Temple apparently knew nothing of the plans for the revolution, he nevertheless moved his family back to Sheen when he found that Moor Park lay between the armies of James and William. King William subsequently made several visits there, and on one of them asked Temple to become secretary of state. For the third time in his life, he declined the honor.

Temple's peaceful retirement at Sheen was shattered in early April, 1689, by the suicide of his only surviving son, John, who had been appointed secretary of war less than a week before. Young Temple had been despondent for some time; although the cause of his depression is not clear, the responsibilities of his office probably were not involved.[9] Temple was heartbroken when he heard the news of his son's drowning in the Thames River; it is likely and understandable that he had hoped that John would be able to carry forward the policies for which he himself had worked. With Lady Giffard, and John's widow, and her children, the Temples returned to Moor Park in the latter part of the year.

Sometime during the year 1689 Jonathan Swift, twenty-one years old and distantly related to Lady Temple, appeared at Sheen to enter Temple's household, where he remained for a major portion of the next decade. During this time he made his first clumsy and unfortunate attempts at poetry; but, when he left Moor Park ten years later, he carried with him the manuscripts of

A Tale of a Tub and *The Battle of the Books,* as well as a headful
of reading derived in Temple's well-stocked library.

The last ten years of Temple's life were quiet ones. As his disap-
pointments slipped further into the past, he found increasing
pleasure in his gardens, his books, and his writing. Although the
faint echoes of political strife rumbled in the distance, Temple
lived in the serenity and peace of Moor Park, working on his
memoirs, writing and publishing a number of essays, and tending
his gardens.

But his end was near. When Lady Temple died in early February, 1695, she was buried in Westminster Abbey beside her
daughter Diane. When Temple himself died four years later,
Swift recorded the event, and his words imply much about his
attitude toward the man to whom he had been so close: "He died
at one o'clock this morning (27th January, 1698–9), and with him
all that was good and amiable among men." [10] Temple was interred beside his wife and daughter in Westminster Abbey; his
heart, in accordance with his instructions in his will, was buried
beside the sundial in the garden at Moor Park.

II *His Thought*

Temple's personality and works have, as we have noted,
aroused either strong sympathy or harsh antipathy. Some critics
have thought him a dull, pedantic dilettante; others, a charming
writer. Some have praised the originality of his thought, while
others have seen him as merely a derivative thinker, and a poor
one at that. Thomas Macaulay was probably right when he called
Temple "a man of lively parts and quick observation, a man of the
world among men of letters, a man of letters among men of the
world. Mere scholars were dazzled by the ambassador and cabinet councillor; mere politicians by the essayist and historian." [11]

But classification, with Temple as with any other human being,
is not so simple, as Clara Marburg has shown in her excellent
study: "Temple was an individual, who must be seen not exclusively as 'a man of the world,' nor even as a 'man of letters,' but
rather as an inquiring, impressionable, not very profound mind,
trying to find a place for itself in the shifting seventeenth-century
world of thought." [12] In his essays, ranging from *An Essay upon
the Present State and Settlement of Ireland* (written before July,
1668) to *Some Thoughts upon Reviewing the Essay of Ancient*

and Modern Learning (composed after 1694), we see rather clearly several strains of seventeenth-century thought: a skepticism toward science, a rejection of the idea of progress, an attraction to the Epicurean ethic, and a championship of the ancients.

The main currents of Temple's thought are fairly clear. To him, the self-assured intellectual pride of the scientists was galling because his own experience and observations had taught him that science could not assure happiness to men. Natural philosophy, he says in his essay *Upon the Gardens of Epicurus* (1685), seemingly has no purposes except those of vanity or snobbery (*Works*, I 172). Neither truth nor happiness, then, can be found in the experiments of the virtuosi. As Miss Marburg observes, Temple stood at the end of a long tradition of Renaissance skepticism embracing such thinkers as Michel de Montaigne, Pierre Charron, Sir Thomas Browne, William Bulstrode, and Blaise Pascal.[13]

Closely related to Temple's skepticism is his rejection of the idea of progress. Believing that men are fundamentally alike in all ages and places and that any notable differences might be attributed to the influence of environment, Temple instead accepts a cyclical theory of history in which, despite periodic fluctuations, man remains relatively unchanged. This attitude toward history motivated Temple's quarrel with the scientists as well as with the critics; and, in the light of his attitude, the essays on gardening and learning must be read.

Another aspect of Temple's thought is his championing of a mild and temperate Epicureanism in the essay on gardens. Thoroughly distrusting the pretension of the natural philosophers, on the one hand, and the mystical speculations of such as the Cambridge Platonists, on the other, Temple found his *summum bonum* in a discreet Epicureanism which reflected his own pleasures. Lady Giffard tells us that he was very much an enthusiast for music, art, gardening, walking, and riding.[14] In the essay on gardens he praises Epicurus for his "tranquility of mind" and "indolence of Body," a philosophy which he found comfortable and soothing during his retirement after the pricks and stings of diplomacy.

The final current in Temple's thought is seen in his involvement in the battle between the ancients and the moderns in the last decade of the seventeenth century. Had his scholarship been a bit more professional, or had he toned down some of his claims of superiority for the ancients, he might have emerged unscathed. We must remember, however, that his espousal of the ancient writers was based less upon his mistaken notion of their greatness than upon his theory of history. Only when seen in light of his historical views can his position in the ancients-moderns quarrel be fully understood. In summary, these attitudes—skepticism, rejection of the theory of progress, a temperate Epicureanism, and championing of the ancients—are the basic ones in Temple's philosophy which must be discussed in this study.

CHAPTER 2

First Flights

RETURNING from his second journey to the Continent in November, 1652, Temple brought with him the manuscripts of a number of essays and romances written during his stay in Brussels. They remained in manuscript until 1930, when G. C. Moore Smith published them in a scholarly edition. Certainly not enduring literary works in any sense, they are nevertheless indicative of the directions in which Temple's interests were tending in the third decade of his life because occasional passages foreshadow ideas found later in the essays of his maturity.

The manuscript published by Moore Smith contains five romances and six essays, plus fragments of six others. Four other romances are not extant. Thus, the *corpus* of Temple's writing by 1652 would, as Woodbridge suggests, "have made a volume of respectable size, and the task of composition must have occupied a good part of the young traveler's time." [1] The titles of the nine romances indicate how deeply Temple was influenced by prevailing tastes: *The Labyrinth of Fortune, The Fate of Jealousy, The Brave Duellists, The Incestuous Pair, The Constant Desperado, The Force of Custom, The Generous Lovers, The Maid's Revenge,* and *The Disloyal Wife.* Similarly, the titles supplied by Woodbridge for some of the essays reveal the tenor of Temple's thought in these early years: *Of the Inconstancy and Variety of Our Judgments, Of Reverie and Idle Fancy, Of Fortune and Content, Of Envy and Jealousy, Of Stained Honor,* and *That Virtue Is Not the Mean of Vices.*[2]

I The Romances

That the romances were written during Temple's courtship of Dorothy Osborne is hardly surprising. The young lady was an inveterate reader of romances, as we learn from her letters to her absent lover. She sends him La Cal prenède's *La Cleópâtre* (1646–

47) volume by volume, but not without apology: "but what an Asse am I to think you bee idle enough at London to reade Romances." [3] Again, she sends him de Scudéry's *Artamène, ou le Grand Cyrus* (1649–53),[4] some fifteen thousand pages in all, and later asks him to "tell mee wch you have most compassion for." [5] Later, she is pleased to learn of his general agreement with her judgments of the romance's characters and plot.[6] At other times she mentions de Gomberville's *Polexandre* (1632), M. de Scudéry's *Ibrahim ou L'illustre Bassa* (1641), Le Maire's *Prazimène* (1643), and Lord Broghill's *Parthenissa* (1654) with varying degrees of pleasure or even, as in the case of *Parthenissa*, distaste.[7]

Clearly, Dorothy was an enthusiast for romances, and Temple's dedication of his own efforts to her is therefore hardly surprising. In his prefatory note, with language appropriate to the situation, he tells her that she has claim to all that comes from his heart, but that its present fruits may not be worthy of her. He then recalls the circumstances under which the romances were composed:

Would I could doe it without calling to mind the pains of that taedious absence, wch I thought never would have ended but with my life, having lasted so much longer then I could ever figure to myself a possibility of living without you. How slowly the lame minutes of that time past away you will easily imagine, and how I was faine by all diversions to lessen the occasions of thinking on you, wch yett cost mee so many sighs as I wonder how they left mee breath enough to serve till my return.[8]

Thus, he found reading about the misfortunes of others a way of sublimating his own: "those books became pleasant to mee wch would have been painful to a better humor, and whilst I pittyed others I sometimes forgott how much I deserved it myself." [9]

But, having read a number of French stories, he found some relief in retelling them, "for I made it the pastime of those lonely houres that my broken sleeps used each night to leave upon my hands. Besides in the expression of their severall passions I found a vent for my owne, wch if kept in had sure burst mee before now, and shewd you a heart wch you have so wholly taken up that contentment could nere find a room in it since first you came there." [10] Since he ostensibly meant these works only for Dorothy, he explains the circumstances that could lead to their publication:

"A friend found them by chance among some other scribled papers from whom all my importunity could never since recover them. When I found hee was resolved to publish them I could not but send this [note] along with them, not thinking it fitt to let any thing of mine goe abroad without the marke of my servitude." [11] The story is rather implausible, but it could hardly have failed to warm Dorothy's heart.

The nine stories are adapted from the French of Francois de Rosset's *Histoires Tragiques*, a volume available to Temple in the editions of 1615 and 1639.[12] Following Rosset's plots rather closely, Temple derived *The Constant Desperado* from the fourth story in Rosset's collection; *The Generous Lovers*, from the sixth; *The Force of Custom*, from the ninth; *The Maid's Revenge*, from the eleventh; *The Disloyal Wife*, from the fifteenth; *The Labyrinth of Fortune*, from the tenth; *The Fate of Jealousy*, from the third; *The Brave Duellists*, from the first; and *The Incestuous Pair*, from the fifth.[13]

The first story, *The Constant Desperado*, develops the theme of constancy in illicit love. Alidor, a renowned soldier of Picardy, and Callirea, the wife of Lycidas, fall in love at first sight. Through their servants, Fatyme and Iris, they exchange letters for a while before Lycidas discovers the affair and takes Callirea to Flanders with him. She dies of a fever; and, upon learning this news from Fatyme, Alidor attempts suicide, but Fatyme prevents him. He goes to the Egyptian desert (though interrupted by his capture by pirates) to worship his dead love and her two pictures (one in life, one in death), and to die of grief.

In *The Force of Custom*, John Vaumorin, a Parisian court tailor, marries Jane Perrot and soon fathers a son, Michel. Suddenly but justly accused of being an accomplice to a man hanged for theft, John is found guilty and sentenced to a galley given by Henry II as a wedding present to his daughter Marguerite and her husband, the Duke of Savoy, The galley is then sold to a Spanish sea captain who takes it to Naples. Years pass; Jane hears no word of her husband, and she tells her son that his father is dead. Michel becomes a singer, and at age twenty-two he travels to Rome in the entourge of a prelate and from thence to Naples. There he visits the galleys and is reunited with his father when he hears the old man's story. Michel seeks his father's liberty from the captain, is at first crudely rebuffed, but succeeds through the

influence of the Duke of Savoy's letter and the surrender of his
last thirty crowns to the captain.

After John gets drunk, they leave for France. On the way, John
picks his son's pockets and continually rails and swears at his condition (all this, Temple asserts, through the "force of ill customs"). Back in Paris, John is reunited with his wife, but not until
he has fought with her second husband, a scrivener, and gone to
court to have the matter settled in his favor. But he continues to
steal; and the theft of a silver bowl at a wedding brings his down-
fall. He is arrested, tried, and hanged—and Temple concludes
with a sermonette on theft: "Honest men esteem hanging but an
ugly kind of death and yet tis that wch theeves straungely affect
and the greatest part of them seem to take it not so squeamishly as
I do a purge. countrys differ in their punishments of other crimes
but in this I thinke all agree as the fittest kind of death for such a
sneaking offence." [14] Temple, like some of his contemporaries, was
almost helpless in the face of a temptation to moralize.

The third tale, *The Generous Lovers*, begins with Temple's
comments on life and death, of which he says, "tis farr easyer to
die well then to live well," and "that wch wee call living or dying
well is in effect nothing else but peoples opinion and esteem of
our carriage in each." [15] When Valeran, a gentleman of Picardy,
falls in love with Amaryllis, she gives in to his demands; and they
live together unmarried, eventually becoming parents of a daughter. All goes well until Valeran quarrels with Aronce, another gentleman, and consequently murders him. The local authorities unsuccessfully try to arrest him, and even the king's forces fail for a
time. The pleas of a cleric and Amaryllis's mother fail to persuade
the couple to surrender. The gate is finally breached, but Valeran
and Amaryllis shoot themselves and fall into a bonfire to avoid
capture—and Temple then moralizes, "thus they livd in flames,
they died in flames, and who knows what became of them after
their deaths." [16]

In the next story, *The Maid's Revenge*, the bloodiest of the five,
Adraste, a hero in the wars against the Turks, returns to France,
marries, and sires a beautiful and talented daughter, Fleuria, who
is at the proper age courted by gentlemen who use their poetry,
wealth, or position to try to win her hand. She falls in love with
young Lucidamor, and he with her, but not before they both
suffer the symptoms of lovesickness: languor, restlessness, and

melancholy. Meanwhile, from Italy appears Chlorizander, who, after visiting Lucidamor and seeing Fleuria's picture, also falls in love with her. Vowing to seduce her or die in the attempt, Chlorizander hires a servant, Modrun, to assassinate Lucidamor, who is soon killed. Fleuria vows to enter a convent; but, before she can do so, Chlorizander's guilt is exposed by another conscience-stricken servant. She then vows revenge, which she effects by luring Chlorizander to a secluded summer house on an amorous pretense, binding him in a net, cutting off his nose, poking out his eyes, slashing his chest, and cutting out his heart, which she holds in her hands as she laments the dead Lucidamor.

Returning home, she takes poison and dies, to be buried with Lucidamor beneath a stone which reads, in part: "Here lyes an unfortunate paire whose hearts love had so ioyned as death could not divorce. their marriage bed was this tombe, where their bodys at length mett whose soules for a long time had nere been asunder. hee was too happy in her love to scape his rivals envy and shee too unhappy in his death to outlive her own griefe." [17]

The last and longest of the five romances is *The Disloyal Wife*. Interspersing the tale with comments on love and parent-child relationships, Temple tells the story of Altomont, brother of a prominent cardinal, who falls in love with Flaminia, a girl of Rome. Against her wishes, her parents conclude the marriage agreement with Altomont, and the wedding is celebrated. But Flaminia cannot forget her true love, Cleanthes, and, when they see each other at a wedding, their love is rekindled. Soon they are corresponding through Lucia, a maid, and then meeting in Flaminia's bedroom, to which Cleanthes gains entrance by a little-used gate. Their secret is told to Altomont by another maid, but his anger and jealousy wane when Flaminia and Cleanthes avoid each other for six months.

When they resume their affair, they plan to kill Altomont. Cleanthes and his man murder Altomont at night. The Cardinal, Altomont's brother, vows revenge; but he prudently decides to wait. After a year, the two marry; in the meantime, the Cardinal is elected Pope; and Flaminia and Cleanthes flee to Venice to escape his jurisdiction. In Venice, Cleanthes becomes an army commander, but retires, ill with fever, to Padua, where he dies. His nephew Timante, inflamed with love for Flaminia but ignored by her, kills another suitor, Adonio; Lucia, Flaminia's brother; and

Flaminia herself. For his crime he escapes hanging because of his noble blood and his service to the state, but he is imprisoned.

The other four romances—*The Labyrinth of Fortune, The Fate of Jealousy, The Brave Duellists,* and *The Incestuous Pair*—have not survived. But the five extant stories clearly indicate the quality at this time of Temple's work. The stories have a few of the merits of the genre and most of its failings. Temple is basically a competent storyteller. Although his characters in each story are few, and completely one-dimensional, they are sufficiently individualized. Furthermore, the plots are generally simple, uncomplicated, and unoriginal.

On the other hand, the romances have many apparent weaknesses. The plots of all five are loose and episodic, like their originals; in *The Disloyal Wife*, for example, the revenge of the Pope, carefully prepared for, suddenly disappears when he dies. The characters are too simply drawn; one may, within a sentence or two of meeting them, immediately classify them as either heroes or villains, white or black, pure or corrupt. Similarly, stock devices predominate in all the stories: the secret entrance, the pining lovers, the brooding revenger, murder, suicide, illicit love. Perhaps worst of all, Temple frequently begins, ends, or interrupts his story with comments on various subjects which are sometimes distressingly dull. Finally, his use of gallicisms and overdrawn conceits detracts from an otherwise blameless style. But most of these weaknesses are as characteristic of the seventeenth-romance as they are of Temple's stories.

Clearly Moore Smith, Temple's editor, is correct in saying that "It is not to be expected that the stories written by a despairing lover of 22 in the small hours of the night to express his own yearnings in a disguised form, stories which once written, were left unrevised, should seem to posterity other than crude and boyish effusions." [18] Had Temple not gone on to greater work, the romances would be even less important than they are. Young Temple was undoubtedly sincere when he wrote in the dedicatory epistole to Dorothy: "There must needs bee a thousand faults in them besides, wch never were mine having not so much as once lookt them over, since they first fell from my hand. You may excuse them if you please; if not the matter is not great." [19] If Dorothy, for whose eyes only they were first written, could excuse their faults, then perhaps we should be somewhat less critical. Their reflection of young Temple's mind and their anticipation of his later work are perhaps more important.

II *The Essays*

If the romances show us one side of the mind and personality of young Temple—the eager and romantic lover whose stories are the result of his ardent love for Dorothy Osborne—the early essays reveal another aspect of the same young man, one possessing, as Woodbridge rightly judges, a "temper ardent, generous and modest; a young mind, eager, curious, active, interested in history, in moral and philosophical problems, above all in its own restless play." [20]

The essays reprinted in Moore Smith's collection in no way rival Temple's later works, but they do foreshadow them in style and content. They also reflect Temple's modest place in the evolution of the English essay, as well as the influence upon him of two earlier masters, Montaigne and Sir Thomas Browne. Their true worth probably lies between Courtenay's extreme statements that "they appear to be school-themes upon a large scale, and, though not destitute for originality, not calculated to be instructive or popular," and that "Some of them display a knowledge of the human mind, and a bold examination of human motives, which the most Scottish of metaphysicians may not despise." [21]

Macaulay, Moore Smith, and Woodbridge have noted the influence of Montaigne in both the style and the content of these essays. Temple was certainly not Montaigne's intellectual equal, but that he admired the Frenchman is clearly shown in an anecdote from his third essay about trying to purchase his works.[22] Woodbridge has noted a number of verbal parallels between these essays and those of Montaigne and Sir Thomas Browne, but none of them is striking enough to suggest direct borrowing.[23]

The greatest similarity to Montaigne can be seen in Temple's very personal tone. He is open, frank, and ardent; like Montaigne, he makes himself the real subject of his essays, and his thoughts lead him where they will. As he indicates in the second essay (which Woodbridge has entitled *Of Reverie and Idle Fancy*):

I find soe little ease and satisfaction by giving my thoughts full scope and liberty of rambling that I must een recall them, but they are past it allready, noe sooner out of hand but out of sight, besides

they take such ayery pathes and are soe light themselves leaving
neither impression nor sent behind them that tis impossible to follow
them by the track of either, will let um go they are not worth an hue
and cry, should my memory overtake them, I question whither shee
would know them at a second interview, though indeed they have all
my markes of folly and lightnesse upon them. . . .[24]

Thus, in several of the essays Temple charmingly wanders rather
circuitously around his theme, usually staying within sight of it
but rarely approaching it closely, and all the while giving us delightful flashes of self-revelation.

We see him, for example, as a worried lover as he frets about a
letter from Dorothy: "I have been all this day, (or rather all this
yeare upon such leaden minutes has it rould away) in an excesse
of perplexity about the miscarriage of a letter, which I would not
stand with the post for though hee should aske mee one of my
eares; the sunn and my hopes of it sett together. . . ." [25] Or he is
jealous: "I have knowne a case, where for the whole earth, I
would not have had my suspition lasted, but for heaven and earth
both I would not have had it prov'd a truth." [26]

Or he is dismayed at his own slowness in learning a foreign
language, a difficulty all the more irritating when compared with
Archduke Leopold's linguistic facility.[27] And yet, like Mark Twain
several centuries later, he ridicules the sounds of German: "Indeed the Allmane is a language I should never learne unless twere
to fright children when they cry, yet methinks it should bee good
to cleare a mans throat that were hoarse with a cold. I have heard
some speak it soe as has made mee expect theire words should
breake down theire teeth as they rush'd out of theire mouth." [28]

Even tobacco offers him a chance to digress at length:

Tobacco gets a man a stomack to his meate and digests what hee
has eaten, tis meate to a poor man and sawce to rich man, it makes a
man melancholly in company and is company to him thats alone, it
makes a sick man well and a well man sick, a sober man drunke and a
drunken man sober, tis an excuse for silence and subject for discourse,
taking it makes a foole passe for a wise man and a wise man for a
foole, by concealing the ones wisdome and suppressing the others
folly, . . . and in fine I should thinke twere an omnipotent thinge
but that *it can't make me take it.*[29]

Despite their discursiveness and their lighter aspects, the essays occasionally foreshadow ideas found in Temple's later work. For example, the religious tolerance of his *Observations upon the United Provinces* (1672–73) is anticipated in an earlier statement in these essays: "methinkes tis too magisteriall even in matters of religion to impose any thinge upon mens beleefe, faith must bee purely an inspiration of heaven or an operation of custome, not a worke either of force or reason, it being out of both their sphears." [30] Clearly, Temple was out of sorts with the fanaticism of the Puritan sects in England and was to find the religious tranquility of Holland more compatible with his own spirit.

He is also an acute observer of men's religious beliefs: "I know some mens faiths are Weathercocks, they turne with every breath, nor that tis in theire power to change theire owne beleefe as they please, for if that were it would bee equally in theire power to fix and keepe it from changing." [31] And elsewhere in these essays he displays an emerging skepticism: "what hounds are wee that with our noses groveling on the earth and sensible objects presume to trace that eternall order and series of thinges, which though it soone leaves us at a loss, yet mounts up by the linkes of a continued chaine the end of which is in the hand of its maker." [32]

Of perhaps more interest to students of literature is the antagonism toward the moderns later manifested in Temple's two essays on ancient and modern learning, but briefly treated in these early works. Some, "impatient of being rival'd" and thinking "they know nothing because others have knowne as much, . . . will endeavour to make others appeare to have knowne lesse then they did. in pursuite of this designe they raise batteryes against those knowne truths, they give assaults where there is no breach, and because they cannot with any likelyhood of successe doe this in a direct line they doe it obliquely. . . ." [33]

And, later, he again attacks the presumption of the moderns: "every foole that cannot comprehend a reason can raise a doubt and as many times a mungrell curr starts a hare which the noble grey-hounds course, so often witty men undertake the patronage of foolish and impertinent opinions either to exercise theire owne wits or our patience, or perhaps to please themselves with making a foole of the world." [34] Four decades of reading and observation were not to change Temple's mind: rigid philosophical systems of any sort were always alien to his temperament.

Nevertheless, the mild Epicureanism of his later essay on gardens is implicit in his early writings on fortune, contentment, virtue, and vice.[35] Most striking, however, is his early defense of Epicurus; he digresses for a moment to defend him against the "vulgar" who have "abus'd this philosophers name by giving it an application so contrary to his customes." [36]

The place of Temple's early efforts in the evolution of the English essay is probably a minor one. Writing less than sixty years after the first translation of Montaigne by John Florio and the publication of the essays of Cornwallis and Bacon, the young Temple produced essays which recalled the Frenchman rather than the Englishmen. Of the earlier seventeenth-century essayists, Sir Thomas Browne seems to be the most congenial to Temple's temperament and style; occasionally there are passages which echo the prose of the Norwich physician. There is little to suggest Browne's direct influence, as Woodbridge would have it found in some rather tenuous parallels,[37] but the immense popularity of *Religio Laici* (1642) may have in some way impressed young Temple. If Temple looks back to Montaigne and perhaps Browne, he also faces forward to the familiar essays of Charles Lamb. The intensely and warmly personal tone of his early works anticipates the same mood in Lamb, whose later praise of Temple is therefore not surprising.

The romances and the early essays, then, are by no means to be placed among Temple's important work. For the most part the stories are the amusements of a young man separated from his beloved, constructed from the stock materials of contemporary fiction with no more important function than that of pleasing a young lady. The essays are better described as collections of notes, rude and as yet unshaped and unpolished. The ideas and interests developed in them were to be refined by Temple's travel, reading, and experience during the next several decades. The youthful methods of the lonesome young man were to be matured as he learned the ways of men and the lessons of history. Twenty years were to pass before Temple appeared in print; during this period, we can safely assume, he was working at his art, reading widely in history and literature, and shrewdly observing the world around him.

CHAPTER 3

Political Theory

IN THE many years remaining to him after the writing of his youthful essays and romances, Temple lived through one of the most exciting eras in modern English history, one which strongly influenced the evolution of modern English government. The lessons of the stormy and perilous years of the civil wars, the regicide, the Restoration, and the Revolution of 1688 were not lost upon him; in a series of works written between 1668 and 1685, he set down his thoughts on the origin of government, its purpose and powers, and its relationship to the governed.

Temple's political ideas are mainly found in two major essays, *Upon the Original and Nature of Government* (written in 1672) and *Of Popular Discontents* (written sometime before 1686). In the first essay, he traces the origin of government to the primitive family; in the second, he analyzes those weaknesses which make people discontented with government. Several other works on government are largely concerned with contemporary problems: *An Essay upon the Present State and Settlement of Ireland* (published 1701); *Upon the Conjuncture of Affairs in October, 1673* (1679); *Observations upon the United Provinces of the Netherlands* (1673); *A Survey of the Constitutions and Interests of the Empire, Sweden, Denmark, Spain, Holland, France, and Flanders* (1679); and *An Essay upon the Advancement of Trade in Ireland* (1679).

I Essays on Government and Political Discontent

The origin of government and political discontent are the focus of Temple's political thought, and it is with them that any discussion of his theories of government should begin; for the other essays are either tangential or supplementary to these two major treatises. *An Essay upon the Original and Nature of Government* opens with the statement of an idea that Temple used again many years later in *An Essay upon the Ancient and Modern Learning:* mankind is very much the same except for certain differences engendered "by the force and influence of the several Climates where they are born and bred; which produce in them, by a different mixture of the Humours and Operation of the Air, a different and unequal Course of Imagination and Passions, and consequently of Discourses and Actions" (*Works,* I, 95).

These variations are responsible for the usual difference among nations in customs, education, and laws; but changes are also effected by foreign and domestic unrest. Nations of climatic extremes, such as "the Regions of *Tartary* and *Muscovy* on the one side, and of *Africk* and *India* on the other," have been characterized by "single and arbitrary Dominions"; on the other hand, those nations situated in the more temperate climates, as in Europe, have tended toward more moderate forms of government. (95).[1]

These governments, according to Temple, are generally of two kinds, one directed "according to the Arbitrary commands and wil of some single Person; and the other according to certain Orders or Laws introduced by agreement or custom, and not to be changed without the consent of many" (95–96). But all forms of government are marked by "restraint upon Liberty; and under all, the Dominion is equally Absolute." Thus, when men cry for liberty, they are in reality seeking "the change of those that Rule, or for the Forms of Government that they have formerly been used to, and (being grown weary of the present) now begin to regret; though when they enjoyed them it was not without some pressure or complaint" (97).

Regardless of the type of government, its two main characteristics are power and authority. Power is synonymous with strength and derives from the governed; authority, which arises from power, resides with the ruler. Authority is not spontaneous; it "arises from the Opinion of Wisdom, Goodness, and Valour in the Persons who possess it." Temple defines wisdom as that quality of mind which helps men to judge "what are the best Ends, and what the best Means to attain them; and gives a Man advantage among the weak and ignorant." Goodness "makes Men prefer their Duty and their Promise before their Passions, or their Interest";

valor "gives Awe, and promises Protection to those who want either Heart or Strength to defend themselves" (98).

An even greater source of authority, however, is the "opinion" of Divine Favour, or Designation of the Persons, or of the Races that Govern," as seen in the kings of the Persians, the Egyptians, the Incas, the Turks, and even the Christian French. Piety, prudence, courage, and custom also strengthen authority because people do not readily distrust men or ideas they have been brought up to believe in, and, therefore, "all Government may be esteemed to grow strong or weak, as the general Opinion of these Qualities in those that Govern is seen to lessen or increase" (99).

In turning to the origin of government, Temple first rejects the social contract theory advanced by Thomas Hobbes in *Leviathan* (1651) and by James Harrington in *The Commonwealth of Oceana* (1656).[2] Such a theory, he believes, is based upon an erroneous conception of man's basic nature:

Some of them lay for their Foundation, That Men are sociable Creatures, and naturally disposed to live in Numbers and Troops together. Others, that they are naturally Creatures of Prey, and in a State of War one upon another; so as to avoid Confusion in the first case, and Violence in the other, they found out the necessity of agreeing upon some Orders and Rules, by which every Man gives up his common Right for some particular Possession, and his Power to hurt and spoil others for the Privilege of not being hurt or spoiled himself. And the Agreement upon such Orders, by mutual Contract, with the Consent to execute them by common Strength and Endeavours, they make to be the Rise of all Civil Government. (99)

However, even if such a contract had once been made, Temple thinks that it would have been negotiated by men who were already rulers of their families: "if we deduce the several Races of Mankind in the several Parts of the World from Generation, we must imagine the first Numbers of them who in any place agree upon any Civil Constitutions, to assemble not as so many single Heads, but as so many Heads of Families, whom they represent, in the framing [of] any Compact or common Accord; and consequently, as Persons who have already an Authority over such Numbers as their Families are composed of" (99–100).

Thus rejecting the social contract, he develops a theory of the patriarchal origin of government which has religious, classical, and Renaissance analogues.[3] According to Temple, the various duties of a father in primitive ages, if adequately performed, were sufficient to make him a ruler over his family: "from all this must arise a great paternal Authority, which disposes his Children . . . to believe what he teaches, to follow what he advises, and obey what he commands" (100).

The father, then, becomes the ruler of the family, which is in reality nothing more than a little state; if he lives long and sires many children, "he grows the Governour or King of a Nation, and is indeed a *Pater patriae*, as the best Kings are, and as all should be." The elder of his children (presumably the son, though Temple does not say so) acquires a degree of authority among the younger and comes to share with his father in "the Consultation and Conduct of their common Affairs." Thus, "A Family seems to become a little Kingdom, and a Kingdom to be but a great Family" (100–101).

Within this petty state, there must be a division of labor; some members are assigned by paternal authority to perform the agricultural activities vital to family survival. Nevertheless, the main responsibility of the father is to provide for the security of property:

what is due to the Servants by Contract, or what is fit for them to enjoy, may be provided, as well as the Portions of the Children; and . . . Whatever they acquire by their Industry or Ingenuity . . . should be as much their Property, as any Divisions of Land or of Stock that are made to the Sons; and the Possession as secure, unless forfeited by any Demerit or Offense against the Customs of the Family, which grow with Time to be the Orders of this little State. (101)

In this primitive state, Temple envisions a monarch as a father who is wise and just in his dealings with his children and servants, and who "advises with his Children in what concerns the Commonweal, and thereby is willingly followed and obeyed by them all." On the other hand, a tyrant is "he that by harshness of Nature, wilfulness of Humour, intemperance of Passions, and arbitrariness of Commands, uses his Children like Servants" (101–2). A further difference between a monarch and a tyrant is found in their attitudes toward armies; a monarch does not need one because he is safe in the love of his subjects, whereas a tyrant thinks he cannot be safe among his Children, but by putting Arms into the hands of such of his Servants as he thinks most at his will; which is the Original of Guards. (102)

The use of a militia, however, is justified against foreign invasion and for defense of national interest. The militia is a citizen army; their "Cause is common Safety; their Pay is Honour"; when they have served their purpose, they return to their homes. But standing armies "are properly Servants armed, who use the Lance and Sword, as other Sevants [*sic*] do the Sickle or the Bill, at the command and will of those who entertain them. And therefore Martial Law is of all other the most absolute, and not like the Government of a Father, but a Master" (102). Temple's distrust of standing armies was shared by many Englishmen in the period after 1660.[4]

Succession in this primitive state is hereditary. The eldest son inherits power and authority if his father has ruled well enough to maintain the confidence and respect of his family (102). But, if for some reason the father loses his authority, the elder or wiser or braver of the sons increases his; and the government is ready for an evolution in form. The sons "succeed in his Authority, whilst the Humour of the whole Body runs against the succession or election of any single Person, which they are grown weary of by so late an Example, and thus comes in what they call an *Aristocracy*" (103).

If, however, the government falls into the hands of a few, it becomes an oligarchy. An additional change evolves when either aristocracy or oligarchy loses its authority: "then the nature of the Government inclines to a *Democracy* or popular State, which is nearest confusion, or *Anarchy;* and often runs into it, unless upheld or directed by the Authority of one, or of some few in the State; though perhaps without Titles or Marks of any extraordinary Office or Dignity" (103).

Temple is wise enough not to describe any one of these types of government as the ideal. Writing in the tradition of the seventeenth-century classical republicans, he says simply, "those Forms are best, which have been longest receiv'd and authorized in a Nation by custom and use. . . . Or else, that those are the best Governments, where the best Men govern; and the difference is not so great in the Forms of Magistracy, as in the Persons of

Magistrates; which may be the sense of what was said of old, (taking wise and good Men to be meant by Philosophers) that the best Governments were those, where Kings were Philosophers, or Philosophers Kings" (104-5).

Government is strongest when it resembles a pyramid with a broad bottom; the base of the pyramid is the "consent of the People, or the greatest and strongest part of them." If the government has majority support, and if "it terminate in the Authority of one single Person, it may likewise be said to have the narrowest top, and so make the Figure of the firmest sort of *Pyramid*." But a government which ignores the opinions, frustrates the interests, and alienates the affections of the people has only a narrow base and is therefore shaky. A monarchy may, therefore, prove to be the best form of government. So also, a government which serves only the interests of the rulers is unstable and subject to frequent upheavals, as demonstrated by evidence from ancient and modern history (105).

The historian of political theory would be hard-pressed to find any significant strains of originality in Temple's essay. Most of his ideas were part of the seventeenth-century intellectual milieu, and Temple's merit lies in his ability to synthesize them into an orderly and readable essay. Despite the passage of almost three centuries, his explanation of the origin of government remains relatively valid, and his analysis of the nature of government, its power, and its authority is still notable for its clarity and common sense.

The companion essay, *Of Popular Discontents,* identifies and discusses the causes of dissatisfactions which afflict governments in any age. At the beginning, Temple says that something in human nature, something which differentiates man from animal, is the cause of civil unrest: "a certain Restlessness of Mind and Thought, which seems universally and inseparably annexed to our very Natures and Constitutions, unsatisfied with what we are, or what we at present possess and enjoy, still craving after something past or to come, and by Griefs, Regrets, Desires or Fears, ever troubling and corrupting the Pleasures of our Senses and of our Imaginations, the Enjoyments of our Fortunes, or the best Production of our Reasons, and thereby the Content and Happiness of our Lives" (I, 256). This restlessness is the source of the dissatisfaction and complaint which "afflict not only our private Lives, Conditions, and Fortunes, but even our Civil States and Governments."

Another source of discontent may be "the unequal condition that must necessarily fall to the Share of so many and so different Men that compose them" (256). From these arise "those Streams of Faction, that with some Course of Time and Accidents overflow the wisest Constitutions of Governments and Laws, and many times treat the best Princes and truest Patriots, like the worst Tyrants and most seditious Disturbers of their Country, and bring such Men to Scaffolds, that deserved Statues, to violent and untimely Deaths, that were worthy of the longest and the happiest Lives" (256–57). As examples of men who suffered at the hands of factions he cites, among others, Solon, Scipio, Hannibal, John DeWitt, Sir Thomas More, Robert Devereux (Essex), and Sir Walter Raleigh (257).

Temple, however, is realistic enough to realize that no age or government is free from these defects, nor will they ever be "till all Men are wise, good, and easily contented" (257). The search for a perfect scheme of government is, therefore, "as endless and as useless a Search, as that of the universal Medicine, or the Philosopher's Stone." But, even if achieved, such an ideal government would eventually decay through accident and time, "and at certain Periods must be furbished up, or reduced to its first Principles, by the Appearance and Exercise of some great Virtues or some great Severities" (258).

Good government, for Temple, is characterized by just laws. Since there exist within every state two divisions, "the innocents" and "the criminals," laws are necessary for social order. Usually these laws reflect community consensus and are at first well executed, but unjust or inefficient execution of them eventually engenders discontent, disorder, and dissension. Temple here restates a maxim from the earlier treatise on government: "those are generally the best Governments where the best Men govern; and let the Sort or Scheme be what it will, those are ill Governments where ill Men govern, and the generally employ'd in the Offices of State" (259). Temple fully realizes, however, the problems of a prince's attempting to choose the best possible officials when men's motives, appearances, and natures are so deceptive. Lacking omniscience, the prince must therefore rely upon his advisers in the selection of his ministers. Furthermore, the government at times may lack talented men in critical situations (259–60).

The greatest danger resulting from the discontents of well-meaning men is that others who are "ill and interessed, and who cover their own ends under those of the Publick, and . . . the Good and Service of the Nation," will take advantage of the desperate situation to promote their own schemes. This chaos in turn leads to sedition, which often destroys effective governments only to replace them with "new Institutions and Forms never intended by those who first began or promoted them"; even worse, sedition may result in tyranny or conquest by another nation (260–61).

Having analyzed the causes of political discontent, Temple proceeds to show how a state should be ruled in order to prevent unrest, sedition, political innovation, and eventual destruction. Ruler and ruled have mutual obligations: "For, as every Prince should govern, as He would desire to be governed if he were a Subject, so every Subject should obey, as He would desire to be obeyed if He were a Prince" (261). There are, however, certain principles by which princes can insure the stability of their states. The first is the avoidance of all innovations 'in Ancient and Establish'd Forms and Laws, especially those concerning Liberty, Property, and Religion"; such continuity in constitutional and legal matters leaves "the Channel of known and common Justice clear and undisturbed."

Second, the prince should serve the "true and common Interest" of the nation without favoring any party or faction; but, if it be absolutely necessary that he make a choice between contending parties, he should "chuse and favour that which is the most Popular, or wherein the greatest or strongest part of the People appear to be engaged." Third, he should introduce and encourage "the Customs and Habits of Industry, . . . for frugal and industrious Men are usually safe and friendly to the establish'd Government, as the Idle and Expensive are dangerous from their Humours or Necessities." And, third, the prince must do all he can to avoid dangerous foreign adventures which create fear at home, making the people jealous of the government and giving them "ill Opinions, either of their Abilities, or their good Intentions" (261–62).

In Section II of his essay Temple demonstrates how these "popular discontents" have harmed England in the past, and he advances certain recommendations for the welfare of the nation. Specifically, he recommends (1) perpetual appropriations for the maintenance of a peacetime navy of fifty capital ships and ten thousand sailors, with provision for an additional thirty ships in war; (2) registration of deeds to encourage commerce; (3) improvement in the administration of public charity; and (4) abolition of the death penalty for theft and for robbery (264–66).

Perhaps just as important are his other recommendations, which he knew his contemporaries would regard as visionary or utopian: (1) the limitation that no man may hold more than one political office or military command at one time; (2) laws encouraging immigration and natural increase of population; (3) a heavy income tax on bachelors over the age of twenty-five; (4) statues controlling dowries and marriage of heiresses; and (5) strengthening of the House of Lords by regulation of the voting age of the peers and restrictions on the creation of new titles (266–70).

Temple says that he offers these proposals in the "true, general, and perpetual Interest of the Nation, without any Regards of Parties and Factions, of the Necessities of particular Times or Occasions of Government." These interests, as he outlines them, are a strong navy, a political balance of power in Europe, and national unity (270).

Believing that "our Nation is too great, and too brave to be ruined by any but it self," he illustrates his distrust of factions by means of an extended ship-state metaphor which is here quoted at length because it so accurately reflects Temple's style:

When a Ship goes to Sea, bound to a certain Port, with a great Cargo, and a numerous Crew who have a Share in the Lading as well as Safety of the Vessel; let the Weather and the Gale be never so fair, yet if in the Course she steers, the Ships Crew apprehend they see a Breach of the Waters, which they are sure must come from Rocks or Sands, that will endanger the Ship unless the Pilot changes his Course: If the Captain, the Master, and Pilot, with some other of the Officers, tell them they are Fools or Ignorant, and not fit to advise; That there is no Danger, and it belongs to themselves to steer what Course they please, or judge to be safe; and that the business of the Crew is only to Obey: If however the Crew persist in their Apprehensions of the Danger, and the Officers of the Ship in the Pursuit of their Course, till Seamen will neither stand to their Tackle, hand Sails, or suffer the

Pilot to steer as he pleases; what can become of this Ship, but that either the Crew must be convinced by the Captain and Officers, of their Skill and Care, and Safety of their Course; or these must comply with the common Apprehensions and Humours of the Seamen; or else they must come at last to fall together by the Ears, and so throw one another over-board, and leave the Ship in the Direction of the Strongest, and perhaps to perish, in case of hard Weather, for want of Hands.

Just so in a State, Divisions of Opinion, though upon Points of common Interest or Safety, yet if pursued to the Height, and with Heat or Obstinacy enough on both sides, must end in Blows and Civil Arms, and by their Success leave all in the Power of the strongest, rather than the wisest or the best Intentions; or perhaps expose it to the last Calamity of a Foreign Conquest. (270)

This essay was written shortly after the difficulties following Popish Plot from 1678 to 1683 and the troublesome accession of James II in 1685; possibly Temple was alluding to current events. At the end of his essay he remarks bitterly, "and thus I have done with these idle politick Visions, and at the same Time with all Publick Thoughts as well as Employment" (271).

These two essays show clearly that Temple was an acute and knowledgeable student of politics. Although most of his ideas were commonplace in their time, his discussion of the patriarchal theory was the best of its kind in the seventeenth century. Frank I. Herriott doubts that Temple's ideas affected contemporary political theory, for his work "seems to have aroused little attention and created but slight comment. It was seed cast upon stony ground." [5]

Nevertheless, his moderate political philosophy and his interest in sound government apparently made his political writings attractive to many, as is shown by the popularity of his essays in the following century. Abel Boyer, his early eighteenth-century biographer, tells us, "He ever was a zealous stickler for the Established Church and Monarchy, and therefore not to be suspected by our modern tories: He was at the same time a constant Enemy to Popery and a French interest; and therefore not obnoxious to the Whigs." [6] Friend and adviser to three kings, Temple retained a lively political curiosity even in his retirement, and the fruits of his observations and experience are displayed to advantage in these two essays.

II *Miscellaneous Political Essays*

The remainder of Temple's political writing is of an occasional nature, works usually written with specific short-range purposes. Among these are his essays on the United Provinces, on Ireland, on the constitutions and interests of the Continental powers, and on the political situation in late 1673. For the most part, these essays consist of Temple's observations upon current problems and his recommendations for their solution or amelioration. Understandably, their popularity has declined greatly as their relevance diminished.

The longest and perhaps most important of these works is the *Observations upon the United Provinces of the Netherlands*, written sometime before November, 1672, and published early the next year (probably in February–March, 1672–73). Composed while England and Holland were at war, the work was probably intended to alleviate the existing difficulties between the two nations, to re-establish their friendship, and to persuade the English ministry to return to the principles of the Triple Alliance.[7] The essay reflects Temple's deep respect for the Dutch and their civilization—a sympathy strikingly uncommon among Englishmen in such a situation.

The *Observations* is a survey of Dutch civilization in which Temple discusses the nation's people and their history, government, religion, economy, and military. The essay is too long for extended analysis here, but a few comments and illustrations will show its tenor and its relationship to Temple's other work. As we might expect, Temple is fascinated by Dutch government, in which he finds many of the qualities he himself believed in but found lacking in England. Although the Dutch people generally are not wise or politically sophisticated, their government, he says, "is . . . composed of the wisest of the Nation; which may give it an advantage over many others, where Ability is of more common Growth" (*Works*, I, 38). And the effectiveness of the Dutch government is enhanced by the careful selection of municipal, provincial, and state officials and even more by "the great Simplicity and Modesty in the common Port or Living of their chiefest Ministers; without which, the Absoluteness of the Senates in each Town, and the Immensity of Taxes throughout the whole State, would never be endured by the People with any patience; being

both of them greater than in many of those Governments, which
are esteem'd most Arbitrary among their Neighbours" (38). The
Dutch go about their public and private business with common
sense, simplicity, moderation, and frugality, traits which Temple
obviously admires.

Perhaps the most noteworthy of his comments are in his chapter
about Dutch religion. He asserts that Protestantism was introduced in Holland as well as in England "by the Operation of Divine Will and Providence" and that, by the same force, Catholicism was retained in France. The tolerant note so characteristic of
his later statements about religion continues as he states that the
religion of a nation should be a spiritual consensus: "'Tis enough,
that God Almighty infuses Belief into the Hearts of Men, or else
ordains it to grow out of Religious Enquiries and Instructions; and
that where-ever the generality of a Nation come by these Means
to be of a Belief, it is by the force of this concurrence introduc'd
into the Government, and becomes the establish'd religion of that
Country" (55).

Anyone who attempts to change the religion of a nation by
other than peaceful persuasion is likely to subject the country to
civil war, tyranny, and their attendant miseries: "Violence, Oppression, Cruelty, Rapine, Intemperance, Injustice, and, in short,
the miserable Effusion of Humane Blood, and the Confusion of all
Laws, Orders, and Virtues, among Men" (55). But religion is also
a matter of individual conscience, whose end, "next to Mens Happiness hereafter, is their Happiness here." By nature, a man has no
more control of his religious beliefs than over his face or physique;
therefore,

A Man that tells me, my Opinions are absurd or ridiculous, impertinent or unreasonable, because they differ from His, seems to intend a Quarrel instead of a Dispute; and calls me Fool, or Mad-man,
with a little more Circumstance; though, perhaps, I pass for one as
well in my Senses as he, as pertinent in Talk, and as Prudent in
Life. . . . But such Language determines all between us, and the
Dispute comes to end in three Words at last, . . . That he is in the
right, and I am in the wrong. (56)

In the United Provinces, freedom of religous belief is granted to
all, except Roman Catholics, so long as their beliefs do not erupt

"into Expressions or Actions of ill Consequence to the State."
Among those enjoying such freedom are the Jews, the Brownists,
the Anabaptists, the Arminians, the Familists, and the Calvinists
(57–58). Consequently, the nation has been relatively free of the
religious convulsions which had afflicted the rest of Europe since
the Reformation.

A third aspect of the *Observations* is Temple's mercantilism—
his belief that a nation's economic well-being is based on a favorable trade balance: "the only and certain Scale of Riches, arising
from Trade in a Nation, is the Proportion of what is exported for
the Consumption of others, to what is imported for their own."
According to Temple's theory, the success of Dutch trade is based
on population density, governmental stability, financial security,
effective justice, efficient transporation, strong business influence
in government, low tariffs, and East Indian colonization (61–65).
Like other Englishmen, Temple was undoubtedly somewhat envi-
ous of Dutch success in overseas commerce. However, the last
chapter of the *Observations* deals with the fall of the United Provinces in 1672, which Temple attributes to the overweening interest of the Dutch in trade to their neglect of military affairs, to
their simplistic trust in defense against land attack, and to some
unfortunate political appointments in the army.

As perceptive as Temple's comments on Dutch civilization
might be, the essay also has its weaknesses. Strangely, in view of
his cultural interests in his other essays, he says little or nothing
about Dutch science, art, or learning. Furthermore, his ventures in
national psychology occasionally prove comic, as, for example, in
his discussion of love among the Dutch: "Their Tempers are not
airy enough for Joy, or any unusual Strains of pleasant Humour;
nor warm enough for Love. This is talkt of sometimes among the
younger Men, but as a thing they have heard of, rather than felt;
and as a Discourse that becomes them, rather than affects them"
(50). Cold and heavy the Dutch might seem, but he stretches the
point too far in this instance.

The *Observations* reflects Temple's knowledge of a country in
which he spent a substantial part of a decade. Although its influence on English relations with the Dutch cannot be determined,[8]
the work was nevertheless popular, going through seven editions
by 1705. Its popularity probably stemmed from its readability and

its worth as a guidebook to a nation in which Englishmen of the time were very much interested for commercial, political, and military reasons.

A second political work is *A Survey of the Constitutions and Interests of the Empire, Sweden, Denmark, Spain, Holland, France, and Flanders,* written sometime before July, 1671; submitted to one of the secretaries of state; and first published in Part I of the *Miscellanea* (1679). Temple's purpose in this work was probably one of persuading the ministry to honor the Triple Alliance; for he begins by pointing out that, although England is militarily strong and geographically isolated, she must still watch the Continental political situation closely because several developments forecast trouble for her: the rapid growth of French military strength, the continued rise of Dutch sea power, and the possibility of an alliance between the Dutch and the French against the English. In the course of the survey which follows, Temple repeatedly calls attention to the danger of French aggression. But most of the essay consists of his comments upon the political interests of the major European nations, which, except in the case of France, rarely run to more than three or four paragraphs.

At the end of the treatise he suggests three possible courses of action for England: (1) "Either to preserve our present Alliances, and thereby the peace of *Christendom* as it now stands." (2) "Or to encourage *France* to an Invasion of *Holland,* with the assurance of our Neutrality." (3) "Or else to join with *France* upon what Advantages they can offer us, for the Ruin of the *Dutch*" (93). His strong advocacy of the first alternative is clear enough as he expresses his reservations about the second and third possibilities, thus affirming his belief that the second is unworkable and the third dangerous. The only criticism he can make of the first is that, in peacetime, France and Holland might become wealthier than England (93–94). Unfortunately, the paper was a failure; King Charles II and his ministers were not interested because Temple's policy was incompatible with their own designs.

A third work of an occasional nature is the essay entitled *Upon the Conjuncture of Affairs in October 1673,* published in *Miscellanea, Part I* (1679). Probably written at the request of the Duke of Ormond, the essay is another of Temple's attempts to persuade the government to resume the former policy of the Triple Alliance

against France. In the opening section of the essay, he briefly analyzes the current situation: an alliance with France in the second
year of a war against the Dutch; the danger of entanglement in a
quarrel between France and Austria; and the possibility of war
with Spain (*Works*, I, 122).

The important issue is England's financial stability. The revenues of the nation may "wither away in a very great Measure"
because of Dutch, French, and, possibly, Spanish interdiction.
With this income gone, financial support of the war must fall
upon the people, whose faith in the nation's ultimate military success assures the financial plans (123–124). But at present the nation is not strongly in favor of war; therefore, because money will
be scarce, King Charles's only choice is to (1) negotiate a peace;
or (2) convince Parliament and people that the war is being
fought upon "Points of Honour, Justice and Safety" that are consistent with national interest and based upon the possibility of a
fair peace. The main issues between England and Holland, as
Temple sees them, are those of the nautical honors rendered to
national flags in the English Channel, a firm agreement on English rights in Surinam, fishing rights for the Dutch near the English coast, and new negotiation of the East India trade. He also
urges an understanding with Spain (124–26).

If these issues are settled, Temple thinks that Charles will benefit both at home and abroad: "Thus much is certain, that whatever
Means will restore, or raise the Credit of His Majesty's Government at Home, will do it Abroad too: For a King of *England* at
the Head of his Parliament and People, and in their Hearts and
Interests, can never fail to making what Figure he pleases in the
World" (127). Ironically, however, he concludes with a statement
that was to prove all too prophetic for Charles II and his succes-
sor, James II: "But in running on Counsels contrary to the general
Humour and Spirit of the People, the King indeed may make His
Ministers great subjects, but they can never make Him a great
Prince" (127). Subsequent events of the troubled years before
1688 were to prove the truth of this statement.

Since the last two of Temple's political essays deal with the
Irish problem, they may be discussed together. The first is *An
Essay upon the Present State and Settlement of Ireland*, written
in 1668 but not published until 1701 in the *Select Letters*. The
other is *An Essay upon the Advancement of Trade in Ireland*,

submitted to the Earl of Essex, lord-lieutenant of Ireland, in July, 1673, and printed in the first part of the *Miscellanea* (1679). In both works, Temple assumes that, despite anything he might suggest, Ireland will continue to be exploited by England; thus he realistically proposes remedies that might ameliorate the deplorable conditions in that country.

The background of the essay on the state and settlement of Ireland is found in the settlement made by Oliver Cromwell and the Rump Parliament in 1652. Cromwell's supporters were given the lands of Irish aristocrats. Many Irish were transplanted to the undesirable lands in less fertile parts of Ireland, while others were "transported" across the seas. When Charles returned in 1660, Ireland was in chaos. Any chance for re-establishing political, social, and economic stability was lost in the clash of political power and private interests after the Restoration.

Although Temple realizes that the fundamental question of Ireland's subordination to England has been settled, he believes that certain new measures might improve Irish administration. Since the king does not derive enough income from the island to pay for its administration, he suggests several improvements: (1) a quit-rent amounting to one-fourth the annual income on all land grants; (2) other land taxes; and (3) a reduction in the size of the military forces garrisoned in Ireland and their subsequent reorganization for closer discipline.[9] Furthermore, only strongly Protestant and loyal Englishmen should be used in the Irish government. A strong ministry might help the situation by attracting Protestant immigrants through a promise of religious tolerance and other rights and by clearing the native Irish from the counties surrounding Dublin and replacing them with patriotic Englishmen.[10]

Clearly, then, Temple does not question the morality of the Cromwellian settlement; and his interest lies in making the best of it. From the twentieth-century point of view he may appear very illiberal, but Temple here, as elsewhere, was interested only in that which was politically feasible. Whatever idealistic notions he may have had about the salvation of Ireland were pragmatically subordinated to the realities of the situation.

In the second essay, which deals with Irish trade and with deplorable conditions which were to continue long after Temple's death, many of his suggestions are reasonable; but few of them were ever put to the test. Near the beginning of his essay Temple states a widely held seventeenth-century theory concerning the relationship of national wealth to population density: "The true and natural Ground of Trade and Riches, is number of People, in proportion to the Compass of Ground they inhabit. This makes all Things necessary to Life dear, and that forces Men to Industry and Parsimony" (*Works*, I, 110).[11] Thus, trade languishes because of the decimation of the Irish population by two plagues and two wars. Furthermore, the instability of Irish politics had caused the emigration of many talented people who might otherwise have lent steadiness to Irish government and finance (110).

Temple proposes a rather long list of stimulants for improved trade: (1) encouragement of the flax and linen industry; (2) expansion of trade in hides, tallow, and butter and improvement of the industry by better cattle husbandry; (3) repeal of the Cattle Act of 1666, which had so severely constrained the Irish cattle industry; (4) development of commercial fishing; (5) establishment of two free ports; (6) passage of forestry laws with a view toward strengthening the shipbuilding industry; and (7) inclusion of two merchants in the Irish Privy Council. On the other hand, English monopolies must not be endangered; thus the laws forbidding export of Irish wool to any nation other than England must be strictly enforced lest English manufacturers suffer (113–21 *passim*).

These two Irish essays are undoubtedly Temple's least-known works, because of their small literary value and their negligible influence on reform. The problems dealt with in these short treatises were to plague Ireland for another two and a half centuries. Nevertheless, the essays do show the workings of a mind alert and sensitive to Ireland's economic and political environment. If Temple did not solve the Irish dilemma, he was no better and hardly any worse than his contemporaries and his successors in the following centuries.

III *The Politics of the Middle Way*

Temple's political works reflect his keen sensitivity to the swift and varying thought currents of his time. Although as a practicing politician he may have been somewhat idealistic in his dealings with an unscrupulous king and a devious cabinet, his two essays on government show a keen understanding of the origins, the types, and the workings of government. Rejecting the social-contract theory as stated by Richard Hooker, James Harrington, Thomas Hobbes, and John Locke, he outlined a patriarchal hypothesis which is relatively sophisticated and modern since it ignores abstractions and relies upon history and observation. And his analysis of the causes of, and the remedies for, political unrest are as timely today as they were when Temple first wrote them.

In his comments on government Temple appears as a moderate Whig whose ideas would have appealed to many reasonable men in the Restoration. Having witnessed the chaos of the 1640's and 1650's, as well as the unsettled conditions of the reign of Charles II, Temple longed for the peace and security which only a stable, broadly based and supported government could bring the nation. Distrustful of both political and religious fanaticism, he rightly felt that the well-being of England depended upon a proper relationship between a ruler and his people and upon guarantees of religious and political freedom. The reckless methods of Charles could only bring disaster, and the rabid factionalism of some of the king's enemies would have similarly dire consequences.

Unfortunately, Temple's comments were ignored by his contemporaries, and his political essays have been forgotten by later generations. In spite of their merits, Temple's thoughts on government did indeed turn out to be little more than "idle politick Visions."

CHAPTER 4

History

ASIDE from the importance of the essays to the understanding of Temple's political thought, those about politics reflect his lifelong interest in history. For him, as for his contemporaries, history had a moral purpose; thus, he used it to document his assertions as well as to record the rise, decline, and fall of various civilizations. Early in his career he begins his *Observations upon the United Provinces* with a long and effective history of the Netherlands; and, in what was probably his last work, *Some Thoughts upon Reviewing the Essay of Ancient and Modern Learning,* he employs history in tracing the decline of learning since ancient times.

Temple, of course was neither a professional nor a prolific historian. His only full-length historical work is *An Introduction to the History of England* (1695; revised edition, 1699), and even this book seems incomplete. But in such works as the second and third parts of the *Memoirs* (published 1691 and 1709, respectively), we find a documentary of his own experiences in the foreign service of King Charles II. Although these works are primarily political history, Temple was also interested in what we today call "cultural history," as evidenced in his essays on learning, on gardening, and on heroic virtue.

In the background of these essays lies Temple's attitude toward history. Rejecting the claim of many of his contemporaries to continuous progress in the arts and sciences, he developed, as we have already noted, his own cyclical theory of civilization. Man does not make infinite and unbroken progress; instead, he remains very much the same in all times and places, and his variations largely stem from the influences of climate and environment. As he looked into the past and surveyed civilization from China to Peru, and as he traced the movement of learning from ancient times to the modern, Temple thought he found conclusive evi-

dence that the progress worshiped by so many of his contemporaries was a chimera. Like classical, medieval, and Renaissance
historians before him, he felt that man could learn from the
lessons of the past. History teaches, and man should read it closely
for solutions to his own problems.

I An Introduction to the History of England

An Introduction to the History of England was published in
1695 and reprinted with revisions in 1699. Although evolution of
the book is not clearly traceable, we do know that Swift helped
Temple prepare it for the press before leaving for Ireland in
1694.[1] Earlier in the year Temple had received an inquiry from
John Dunton as to his willingness to assist in the publication of a
history of England. Temple declined, but nevertheless advanced
some suggestions for rewriting extant histories of earlier reigns,
among them More's Edward IV, Edward V, and Richard III; Bacon's Henry VII; Lord Herbert of Cherbury's Henry VIII; Sir
John Hayward's Edward VI; and Camben's Elizabeth.[2] Rejecting
the plan on legal grounds, Dunton dropped the project.

However, on February 14, 1695, Temple wrote to a "Mr. Bentley, bookseller, in Covent Garden," repeating almost verbatim the
plan proposed to Dunton, but adding that such a history would
have the advantage of historians "who lived near the reigns which
they write of, and were some of the wisest, the greatest, or the best
acquainted with affairs of any in their own time." On the other
hand, a newly written history "will either take up many years doing, or will prove but a second edition of Sir Richard Baker
[*Chronicle of the Kings of England*]. Some hand of note will take
up the method you slight, and then a mercenary pen will never
bear a second impression." [3] Bentley also declined the proposal,
but Temple shortly thereafter published *An Introduction to the
History of England*.

Other than these facts, we know little. Woodbridge is correct in
believing that Temple probably wrote the history with a view toward using it as an introduction to the general history of England
which he proposed to Dunton and Bentley,[4] for Temple remarks
that the English have not yet written, but need, a "good or ap-
proved" history of their nation which can compete with the national histories of such Continental historians as Jean des Serres,
Francois de Mezeray, Juan de Mariana, and Pedro de Mexia. Eng-

lish historians have written works that are so "tedious" in their narratives, "injudicious" in their selection of facts, and "wretched" in their styles that the reader is apt to yawn. After referring to his earlier scheme of compiling the histories of earlier writers, he admits that he had at one time considered writing an abridged history, but that, pressed by other work, he had unsuccessfully encouraged others to undertake the task. Thus, he published the present work to *"invite and encourage some worthy Spirit, and true Lover of our Country"* to complete it (*Works*, II, 527–28).

In the preface, he tells us that his plan in his *Introduction to the History of England* is to put forward *"a short Account of this Island, the* Names, *the* Inhabitants, *and* Constitutions *thereof, from the* first Originals, *as far as I could find any Ground of probable Story, or of fair Conjecture, since* Philosophers *tell us,* That none can be said to know Things well, who does not know them in their Beginnings" (528). The history as written follows this outline closely. Temple begins with a short discussion of the origin of the names Britain and Scotland, and then proceeds to a description of the government, religion, and society of the pre-Roman tribes. He then traces the successive invasions of the Romans, the Angles and Saxons, the Jutes, and the Danes. The Anglo-Saxon period is covered so sketchily that, strangely enough, the momentous reign of Alfred the Great is covered with less than twenty words. The remainder of the book, amounting to about three-fourths of the printed text, is devoted to the Norman invasion of 1066 and to the reign of William the Conqueror. The work concludes with Temple's lengthy analysis of the character and policy of William and his influence on the English nation.

The book is thus disproportionate and to that extent unsatisfactory, and Temple exhibits scholarly weaknesses which occasionally mar his other work: ignoring the unfamiliar, generalizing, and guessing rather than investigating. In his defense, however, it must be remembered that he was writing in an age which had not yet recovered the many and useful sources and research tools which modern Anglo-Saxon scholars take for granted. Thus the errors indicated by David C. Douglas are somewhat mitigated.[5] Temple's treatments of the religious history of William's reign, of the Anglo-Norman jury system, and of feudalism are somewhat inaccurate, and Douglas concludes that "He had neither the knowledge nor indeed the inclination to make a proper examina-

tion of the materials for his study, and his essay failed of its purpose for that very reason." [6] Because there is no clear evidence
as to his sources, Temple's errors must be judged with charity.
Woodbridge, who has shown very clear parallels between
Temple's history and Samuel Daniel's *First Part of the History of
England* (1613), may be right in believing that Temple "wrote
with Daniel's book before him, or close at hand." [7] These parallels
are strikingly close, but not sufficiently so to establish clearly the
degree of his dependence on Daniel. It is more likely that he used
Daniel's history as an occasional reference, as he did George Bu-
chanan's *Rerum Scoticarum Historia* (1582), Aylett Sammes's *Bri-
tannia Antiqua Illustrata* (1676), and Milton's *History of Britain*
(1670). Whether Temple made use of the Tudor chronicles is not
certain, but Woodbridge thinks that he knew them but did not
use them.[8] The truth is that Temple probably, as usual, selected
whatever materials were conveniently near; he was not a professional scholar, as his unfortunate experience with Aesop and Phalaris in the ancients-moderns controversy had clearly shown five
years before the publication of this history.

Although Temple probably wrote the book to encourage some-
one else to complete a general history of England, both Woodbridge and Douglas suggest that he may have had another purpose in mind: the justification of the Revolution of 1688 and the
coronation of William of Orange as king of England. This suggestion is strongly based on internal evidence and the long association of the two men. Temple's acquaintance with the Prince of
Orange began in late August or in early September of 1668,
shortly after his appointment as ambassador to The Hague; and
they remained friends for the rest of their lives. As we have noted,
William approached Temple in April, 1676, and asked his opinion
about the feasibility of a marriage to Mary Stuart; Ultimately, the
match was secured through Temple's efforts and negotiations, and
the marriage took place in November, 1677. In the remaining
years of his life, Temple advised him on the Exclusion Bill of 1680
and received a number of visits from the new monarch at Sheen in
1689, but he declined to become his secretary of state. The two
men exchanged additional visits during the next decade; and, as
we shall see, Temple made William the hero of the second part of
his *Memoirs*.

Thus it is hardly surprising that Temple was tempted to draw flattering parallels between his friend and William the Conqueror, both foreigners who ascended the English throne and who were forced to assert their right in the face of strong challenges. That Temple was attempting to justify and popularize William's reign seemed plainly evident to Temple's early biographer, Abel Boyer:

It was the general opinion that Sir William Temple, who continued to the last a true friend to the Prince of Orange, the late King William of ever-glorious memory, published at this time his Introduction to the History of England, both to compliment that Prince, under the character of the Norman Conqueror, which he draws and sets off to great advantage, and to assert the late Revolution, by showing that Edgar Atheling, who had an undoubted right of succession to the crown, was twice laid aside.[9]

William was by no means popular with Englishmen in 1695 when the history was first published; the death of Mary late in the preceding year had made his position much less secure.

Woodbridge's evidence of Temple's purpose needs only summarization here: (1) Temple describes William the Conqueror and his reign at greater length than does Daniel, his major source, and paints a stronger picture of his character; (2) he ignores or glosses over the less palatable aspects of William's reign and person; and (3) he attempts in his conclusion to show that the benefits of William's rule outweighed the shortcomings.[10] As Woodbridge says, "Temple's main justification for his history would be that he had somewhat idealized Daniel's portrait of William, and retouched it in such a way as to bring out the resemblances of the Conqueror to William III, and that similarly he altered the emphasis in his account of William's reign so as to make clear the analogous advantages to England of the Orange succession."[11] If an apologia for William were indeed Temple's purpose, the book is impressive enough, though its political impact is unclear.

Aside from its apparent propagandistic purpose, the *Introduction* takes its place in the increasing number of Anglo-Saxon studies which appeared in the late seventeenth century. As Douglas indicates,

Between 1660 and 1700 English scholars brought to its proper culmination the longest and most prolific movement of medieval research which this country had ever seen. Thus, Anglo-Saxon studies have never, perhaps, advanced with greater rapidity than during these years, and at the same period Anglo-Norman history was being profitably investigated by a large group of devoted students.[12]

It was during the latter years of Temple's life, for example, that William Sommer compiled the first Anglo-Saxon dictionary, *Dictionarium Saxonico-Latino-Anglicum* (1659); that George Hickes wrote the first Old English grammar, *Institutiones Grammaticae Anglo-Saxonicae et Maeso-Gothicae* (1689); and that Robert Brady produced his *Introduction to the Old English History* (1695).

Temple's attempt at English history, despite its shortcomings, reflects the renascent interest of his century in the wellsprings of English civilization. Unfortunately, he was ill-equipped to make a more solid and lasting contribution; a more prudent scholar such as Richard Bentley or William Wotton probably would have avoided his errors. Nevertheless, unmarred by the heavy hand of the academician, *An Introduction to the History of England* occupies an important place in Temple's works, for it reveals the facility of his mind, the fluency of his style, and the tolerance and breadth of his historical perspective.

II Memoirs

As a historian of contemporary political affairs, Temple is even more enlightening. The record of his diplomatic work is found largely in his *Memoirs*, although a detailed analysis of his career abroad would also have to take into account his voluminous correspondence. He probably wrote his *Memoirs* in three parts: Part I, according to Swift, was deliberately burned in manuscript; Part II was begun in April, 1687, and printed in 1691; Part III was started in February, 1681, but was not published until 1709.

Temple began writing his *Memoirs* very shortly after his retirement from public affairs. Part II is entitled *Memoirs of What Past in Christendom from the War Begun 1672 to the Peace Concluded 1679*. In the prefatory epistle Temple promises his son that he will, if he himself lives, leave him "some *Memoirs* of what has pass'd in my publick Imployments, especially those abroad, which reach'd from the Year 1665, to 1678; and run through the most important foreign Negotiations of the Crown, with great Connexion of Affairs at home during this Period, and the Revolutions it produc'd" (*Works*, I, 373).

He comments that his connections with the king and his ministers have given him "the Advantage to discern and observe the true Springs and Motions of both; which were often mistaken in Court and Parliament, and thereby fasten'd many suspicious, Confidences, Applauses, Reproaches, upon Persons, and at Times, here they were very underserv'd" (373). After reviewing his career and his motives, he closes his preface by saying that because only his love for his son could motivate him to write such a work, he desires that it not be published during his lifetime.

Part II traces the later years of Temple's diplomacy. In this section the tone is less defensive than it was to be in Part III, and his enjoyment of his work is evident in his narrative and descriptive passages. Temple is captivating in his descriptions of Nimeguen and its environs (419), a terrible storm (386), the murder of the Dewitts (380–81), and his journey from The Hague to Nimeguen in bitter winter weather:

The Snow was in many Places where I pass'd near Ten Foot deep, and Ways for my Coach forc'd to be digg'd through it; several Postboys dy'd upon the Road; and it was ridiculous to see People walk about with long Icicles from their Noses. I pass'd both the *Rhine* and the *Waal*, with both Coaches and Waggons, upon the Ice; and never in my Life suffer'd so much from Weather as in this Journey, in spight of all Provisions I cou'd make against it. (477)

Temple is a master of narration; the unwinding thread of his story spins out rapidly as he employs anecdotes and character sketches to speed and lighten his story. Interwoven into his narrative are several character sketches which are important because they deal with people whom he knew and understood. Particularly valuable are the portraits of Charles II and William of Orange. The two kings are never directly contrasted, but Temple's belief in the superiority of the Dutchman is clearly evident. William's bravery, determination, and honesty are in sharp contrast to the duplicity and vacillation of Charles II.

Woodbridge is probably right in believing that Temple intended William to be the real hero of the book, and that he also intended to work to picture the Prince of Orange as the defender

of Protestantism against the French Catholic Louis XIV.[13] This
intent would explain the book's publication in 1691, when the
king was in disfavor with many Englishmen who thought of
him as a foreigner:

his chief purpose in printing the *Memoirs* was to render timely aid to
the popularity of his friend and king. He had declined to assist William
by accepting public office; but he could and did help him by means
of his pen. It would not be a wild guess that at some of those visits
paid to Temple by the king the matter was discussed between them.
Probably he suppressed his name in the early editions of the work
because he preferred that some of his old acquaintances who appeared in it should suppose it published without his consent.[14]

Among those who probably would not have enjoyed the publication of the book, had he lived to read it, was Sir Leoline Jenkins,
Temple's colleague at the Congress of Nimeguen. Inexperienced
and pusillanimous in his diplomatic efforts, he probably well deserved the delightful description Temple gives of him as one who

was in perpetual Agonies (as his Word was) after he was left alone in
that Station; having ever so much Distrust of his own Judgment, that
tho' he had the greatest Desire that cou'd be to do well, yet he many
Times cou'd not resolve how to go about it; and was often as much
perplex'd about the little Punctilioes of Visit and Ceremony that were
left to busy that Ambassy, as if greater Affairs had still attended it.
(451)

Temple, too, was plagued by protocol and ceremony (421–25),
but his reaction was certainly less fretful than Sir Leoline's.
    Part III of the *Memoirs* differs from Part II in both content and
style. The second part is largely concerned with Temple's diplomatic career, but Part III treats the English political situation
from 1679 to 1681, the subtitle perhaps indicating Temple's purpose: "Written for the Satisfaction of my Friends hereafter, upon
the Grounds of my Retirement, and Resolution never to meddle
again with any Publick Affairs from this present February, 1680–
81" (*Works*, I, 331). Temple busies himself with the complex and
shifting political interplay in the problem of the Exclusion Bill,
and in the end he justifies his retirement from public life:

I concluded in cold Blood, that I could be of no further Use or Service to the King my Master, and my Country, whose true Interests I always thought were the same, and would be both in Danger when they came to be divided, and for that Reason had ever endeavour'd the Uniting them; and had compass'd it, if the Passions of some few Men had not lain fatally in the Way, so as to raise Difficulties that I saw plainly were never to be surmounted. Therefore upon the Whole, I took that firm Resolution, in the End of the Year 1680, and the Interval between the *Westminster* and *Oxford* Parliaments, never to charge my self with any publick Employments; but retiring wholly to a private Life, in that Posture take my Fortune with my Country, whatever it should prove. (358–59)

Having resolved to quit politics and diplomacy forever, Temple warns against factionalism and expresses the two aims of his own involvement in domestic politics: to preserve the greatness of the monarchy and to establish a revenue to support a strong fleet. He laments, however, "But these have both fail'd, and I am content to have fail'd with them" (359).

Part III, because of its defensive tone, seems of less pertinence to the modern reader than Part II. Moreover, the third section is largely a straightforward narrative devoid of the character sketches and descriptive passages which enliven the second one. Neither work can be rated among Temple's better writing, but both have some relevance as historical documents of the Restoration. If they have any importance in English literary history, it is that they are perhaps the first political memoirs in England. Swift makes such an assertion in his preface to Part III:

'Tis to the French (*if I mistake not*) *we chiefly owe that manner of Writing* [i.e. memoirs]; *and Sir* William Temple *is not only the first, but I think the only English-man* (*at least of any Consequence*) *who ever attempted it.* (329)

Swift's assertion has more recently been substantiated by H. V. Routh.[15] Whereas the essays on government and the history of England show us Temple as a theorist, the *Memoirs* reveal a retired politician reviewing his career and seeking to assess its meaning.

III   Of Heroic Virtue

The essay *Of Heroic Virtue* (published 1690) ostensibly deals with the definition of the term in its title, but it is really a historical work in which Temple surveys several civilizations which were somewhat exotic in the eyes of most of his contemporaries: China, Peru, Scythia, and Arabia. The influence of numerous seventeenth-century works has been noted by Woodbridge and Marburg.[16] In travel and history books by Athanasius Kircher, John Neiuhoff, Marco Polo, F. Alvarez Semedo, Gabriel de Magaillans, Intorcetta, and Arnoldus Montanus, among others, Temple found ample documentation for his cyclical view of history and for his belief that men are very much the same in all times and places. Thus the essay complements the essay on ancient and modern learning published in the same year.

At the beginning of the essay, Temple says that heroic virtue, or political genius, arises from "some great and native Excellency of Temper or Genius" which surpasses the average in "Wisdom, Goodness and Fortitude." These advantages—if complemented by birth, education, and good fortune—serve to make their possessors seem almost divine in the eyes of lesser men, and, as a result, they are "Honoured and Obey'd in their Lives, and after their Deaths Bewailed and Adored." The wisdom of these leaders is manifested in the establishment of laws and governments "as were of most Ease, Safety and Advantage to Civil Society." But they were also brave men who defended their people at home from factions and abroad from enemies; and, by innate genius, they brought effective government to their less civilized neighbors and relieved others from oppression (*Works,* I, 191).

Temple points out that in older cultures these political and military geniuses were deified:

Among the simpler Ages or Generations of Men, in several Countries, those who were the first Inventers of Arts generally received and applauded as most necessary or useful to Human Life, were Honoured Alive, and after Death worshipped as Gods. And so were those, who had been the first Authors of any good and well instituted Civil Government in any Country, by which the Native Inhabitants were reduced from Savage and Brutish Lives, to the Safety and Convenience of Societies, the Enjoyment of Property, the Observance of Orders, and the Obedience of Laws; which were followed by Security, Plenty, Civility, Riches, Industry, and all Kinds of Arts. (192)

As examples of ancient heroes who were raised to divinity by following generations, he cites, among others, Hercules, Theseus, Minos, Achilles, Lycurgus, Romulus, Cyrus, Alexander, and Caesar (192–96).

At the end of Section I, Temple indicates that he will trace the history and workings of heroic virtue in "four great schemes of Government or Empire, that have sprung and grown to mighty Heights, lived very long, and flourished much in these remote (and as we will have it, more ignoble) Regions of the World" (196). Thus he bypasses the more famous civilizations of antiquity (Greece, Rome, Persia, and Assyria) to examine four nations of more exotic attraction: China, Peru, Scythia, and Arabia.

In the second section of the essay he turns to China and its civilization. After a rapid geographical description of the country, its political divisions, its great wall, and its chief city, Peking, he writes of "two great Heroes" of the Chinese: Fohu, the founder of the kingdom, and Confuchu (Confucius) the "most Learned, Wise and Virtuous" of the Chinese. These two men embody the heroic virtue defined at the beginning of the essay. According to Temple, Fohu "introduced Agriculture, Wedlock, Distinction of Sexes by different Habits, Laws and Orders of Government; He invented Characters, and left several short Tables or Writings of Astronomy, or Observations of the Heavens, of Morality, of Physick, and Political Government" (199). These inventions, in turn, cleared the way for advances in Chinese philosophy, science, and agriculture.

Temple is more intrigued, however, with Confucius. He briefly traces the career of the philosopher and comments upon his ethical writings:

The chief Principle he seems to lay down for a Foundation, and builds upon, is, That every Man ought to study and endeavour the improving and perfecting of his own Natural Reason to the greatest Height he is capable, so as he may never (or as seldom as can be) err and swerve from the Law of Nature . . . : That this being not to be done without much Thought, Inquiry and Diligence, makes Study and Philosophy necessary; which teaches Men what is Good and what

is Bad . . . : That in this Perfection of Natural Reason consists the
Perfection of Body and Mind, and the utmost or supreme Happiness
of Mankind. That the Means and Rules to attain this Perfection, are
chiefly not to will or desire any thing but what is consonant to his
Natural Reason, nor any thing that is not agreeable to the Good and
Happiness of other Men, as well as our own. To this end is prescribed the constant Course and Practice of the several Virtues, known
and agreed so generally in the World; among which, Courtesie or
Civility, and Gratitude, are Cardinal with them. In short, the whole
Scope of all *Confutius* has writ, seems aimed only at teaching Men to
live well, and to govern well; how Parents, Masters and Magistrates
should rule, and how Children, Servants and Subjects should obey.
(200)

Temple praises the sage for his wisdom, his wit, and his style; and
he characterizes him as a man "of a very extraordinary Genius, of
mighty Learning, admirable Virtue, excellent Nature, a true Pa-
triot of his Country, and Lover of Mankind" (200).

As in his other writings, Temple is concerned with more than
moral philosophy; and he discusses the more pragmatic aspects of
Chinese civilization—in particular, education and government.
He admires Chinese learning for its lack of pedantry, its
pragmatism, and its efficiency in producing able rulers. As for the
learned, "their Learning and Virtue make them esteemed more
able for the Execution and Discharge of all Publick Employments,
than the longest Practice and Experience in other Countries"
(202).

Turning to ancient Chinese government, Temple observes that it
was an absolute monarchy but nevertheless a political system in
which the advice of several councils was closely followed in choos-
ing men for office. Having analyzed the structure and function of
these councils at some length, he concludes that "it were endless
to enumerate all the excellent Orders of this State, which seem
contrived by a Reach of Sense and Wisdom, beyond what we
meet with in any other Government of the World; but by some
few, the rest may be judged" (203). The endurance of the Chinese government is proved by its stability and strength in the face
of repeated invasions from abroad and civil wars at home (204-
5). As he nears the end of the second section, Temple finds the
only weakness among the Chinese to be "their gross and sottish

Idolatry," which, fortunately, is practiced only among the "Vulgar and Illiterate," whereas the learned worship "the Spirit of the World" without using temples, idols, or priests (205).

Having dealt with China, Temple moves eastward in Section III to Peru. He begins with the discovery of the New World and some comments on Mexico and then passes on to a discussion of Peruvian civilization after the coming of Mango Copac and his sister Coya Mama to civilize the aborigines who lived "without any Traces or Orders, Laws or Religion." As in his account of China, Temple is fascinated by the varying aspects of Peruvian society, most of whose origins are to be found in the teaching and example of Mango Copac. In this society the unifying and under-lying rule was "That every Man should live according to Reason, and consequently, neither say nor do any thing to others, that they were not willing others should say or do to them" (207).

Here Temple finds further evidence that men vary little from one age and nation to another. The government of the Incas was based on reason and ruled with "Justice, Mercy, Piety, Clemency, and Care for the Poor" with the result that " 'Tis certain no Government was ever established and continued by greater Examples of Virtue and Severity, nor any ever gave greater Testimonies, than the *Ynca's,* of an excellent Institution, by the Progresses and Successes, both in the Propagation and Extent of Empire, in Force and Plenty, in Greatness and Magnificence of all publick Works" (208).

Incan religion is similarly impressive. Although the vulgar and unlearned worshipped the sun, the sages taught that the sun was merely the "great minister" of a deity named Pachacamac, the *animador del mundo,* or in Temple's words, *"He that animates or enlivens the World"* (210). His survey of ancient Peruvian civilization ends with a reassertion of his thesis:

that human Nature is the same in these Remote, as well as the other more known and celebrated Parts of the World. That the different Governments of it are framed and cultivated by as great reaches and strength of Reason and of wisdom, as any of ours, and some of their Frames less subject to be shaken by the Passions, Factions, and other Corruptions, to which those in the middle Scene of *Europe* and *Asia* have been so often and so much exposed. That the same causes produce every where the same Effects, and that the same Honours and

Obedience, are in all places but Consequences or Tributes paid to the same Heroick Virtue, or Transcendent Genius, in what Parts soever, or under what Climates of the World it fortunes to appear. (210–11)

The fourth section of the essay deals with the northern region which Temple calls Scythia, the great land mass bounded by the Pacific Ocean on the east and the North Sea on the west, including Scandinavia. After tracing the course of the Scythian conquests and their general southward direction (211–12), he digresses for a moment to discuss the great conquests of Tamerlane, "a Great and Heroick Genius, of Justice, exact Discipline, generous Bounty, and much Piety, adoring one God, tho' he was neither Christian, Jew, nor Mahometan" (212). Temple then examines the civilization of the Scythians. He identifies the area between the Volga and Dnieper rivers as:

the vast Hive out of which issued so many mighty Swarms of Barbarous Nations, who under the several Names of *Goths, Vandals, Alans, Lombards, Huns, Bulgars, Francs, Saxons,* and many others, broke in at several Times and places upon the several Provinces of the *Roman* Empire, like so many Tempests, tore in pieces the whole Fabrick of that Government, framed many new ones in its room, changed the Inhabitants, Language, Customs, Laws, the usual Names of Places and of Men, and even the very Face of Nature where they came, and planted new Nations and Dominions in their room. (212)

Temple suggests that the impetus behind this and other conquests, as well as resultant political institutions, was more than military prowess; instead, he says, they evolved by "some force of Order, some reach of Conduct, as well as some Principle of Courage above the Common Strain" (213). Perhaps, he believes, it was their despising of death, as described in Lucan's *Pharsalia* (I, 458–62).[17]

As the exemplar of heroic virtue among the Scythians Temple chooses Odin, who led his Goths northwestward to the Baltic regions. He credits Odin with being the inventor, or at least the first engraver, of runes; and he also describes him as one who "instituted many excellent Orders and Laws, made the distinction of Seasons, the divisions of Time, was an invincible Warrior, a wise Law-giver, loved and obeyed during Life by his Subjects, and after his Death adored as one of their three chief Gods" (215).

But from the civilization of the Goths, Temple draws three "extraordinary" and "peculiar" principles: their religion, their learning, and their government.

In their religion, the Scythians exhibited a strong belief in an immortality which rewarded the dead in battle with a luxurious life in the palace of Odin, the lazy with an existence in "vast Caves . . . , all dark and miry, full of noysom Creatures usual in such Places, and there for ever grovelled in endless Stench and Misery" (215). And, as evidence of how strongly this concept had permeated the thinking of the Scythians, Temple reprints two stanzas of the death song of Ragnor Lodbrok from the *Literatura Runica* of Olaus Wormius, which Temple admires for its poetic qualities, all the more praiseworthy in light of "the Allowance of different Climates, Fashions, Opinions, and Languages of such distant Countries" (216). This attitude toward death stimulated the people to be "perpetually in new Motions or Designs, fearless and fierce in the Execution of them, and never caring in Battle to preserve their Lives, longer than to increase the Slaughter of their Enemies, and thereby their own Renown here, and Felicity hereafter" (217).

The learning of the Scythians was the second source of their greatness. All of their learning was applied either "to the Knowledge and Distinction of Seasons, by the Course of the Stars, and to the Prognosticks of the Weather," or, on the other hand, to the poetic praise of virtue and valor. The poets were honored by prince and commoner alike, much as were their descendants in seventeenth-century Ireland and Hungary. The minstrels thus served an important function in society: "they rewarded the Prowess of the Old Men among them, and inflamed the Courage of the Young, to equal the Boldness and Atchievements of those that had traveled before them in these Paths of Glory" (217–18).

The third wellspring of Scythian strength was effective government, its form basically derived from the military organization: a leader or general with commanders of divisions forming a council of war and general assembly of troops. The successful leader of such an expedition thus became the prince, who in turn divided the conquered lands among the leaders (the larger shares) and the soldiers (the smaller) who had assisted him in his victory; from this practice arose the feudal political and social structure. Temple digresses for several paragraphs to trace the etymology of the words *baron* and *feudal,* a matter for which he supplies no conclusive answer (218–19). However, there is little doubt in his mind that this Gothic form of government entered every nation subdued by the conquerors. The principle of representation evolved from the ownership of land: "I am apt think [*sic*] that the Possession of Land was the original Right of Election or Representative among the Commons, and that Cities and Boroughs were entitled to it, as they were possess'd of certain Tracts of Land, that belonged or were annexed to them" (220).[18] He concludes with a comment reminiscent of his two major essays on government: a state will never be much troubled by factions if it is "grounded upon the general Consent and Satisfaction of the Subjects"; otherwise, it must rely on force (220).

The fifth section is a discussion of the Mohammedan or Arab civilization which, he says, was "built upon Foundations wholly Enthusiastic, and thereby very unaccountable to common Reason, and in many points contrary even to human Nature" (220). The first part of this section traces the rise of Mahomet and his religion, the authenticity of which is doubtful because "*Mahomet* was subject to Fits of an Epilepsie. . . . He was ashamed of his Disease, and to disguise it from his Wife and Family, pretended his Fits were Trances into which he was cast at certain Times by God Almighty, and in them instructed in his Will, and his true Worship and Laws, by which he would be served; and that he was commanded to publish them to the World, to teach them, and see them obey'd" (221).

Briefly surveying Moslem doctrine, Temple believes that it was designed by the prophet to please Christian heretics (the Arians, in particular), Jews, and the heathen. Its embodiment in the Koran, revered by Mahomet's disciples as sacred, "looks like a wild Fanatick Rhapsody of his Visions or Dreams, or rather of his Fantastical Imagination and Inventions" (222). Nevertheless, by word and sword the new religion swept all before it as it moved into the west and east. Temple attributes the emergence of the Turks as a political and military power to the eight principles undergirding their government: the religion of Mahomet; a belief in the divine right of the Ottomans; the division of conquered lands into sections held only for life or the pleasure of the ruler; the lack of hereditary titles; the suppression of learning; the establishment of the Janizaries; the dietary simplicity and temperance of the army; and the efficiency of justice (224–25).

In spite of their greatness, the Turks, too, lost their initiative and impetus. Temple finds the causes of their decline in the increasing corruption of the Janizaries and their mutinies; the neglect of naval power; and the increasing use of opium. This pattern is natural: empires "like natural Bodies, grow for a certain Time, and to a certain Size, which they are not to exceed," but both internal and external causes may hasten the decline. The "external" reason in the case of the Turks was their encounters with national and racial barriers strong enough to resist them: the Germans, the Tartars, the Persians, and the Ethiopians (226–27).

Despite the later corruption of the Turks, Temple finds some indications of heroic virtue in such leaders as Almanzor, Saladin, Ottoman, and Soliman. In "Justice to the Nobler Nations," however, Temple also lists the great exemplars of heroic virtue among European nations from Epaminondas onward, among them Scipio, Mark Anthony, Alaric, Charlemagne, Gustavus Adolphus, Richard I and Henry V of England, and Temple's friend, William of Orange: "And so I leave this Crown of never-fading Laurel, in full view of such great and noble Spirits, as shall deserve it, in this or in succeeding Ages. Let them win it and wear it" (228).

The sixth and final section deals generally with conquests, their causes, and their effects, from which Temple draws three conclusions: (1) their general direction has been from North to South, as amply proven in the victories of Assyrians, Persians, Macedonians, Romans, Tartars, and Goths over their southern enemies; (2) the less numerous invaders have generally conquered their more populous opponents; and (3) the conquerors have relied more on infantry than on cavalry (229–31). The first two conclusions "may be attributed to the Constitutions of Mens Bodies who compose the Armies that Atchieve them, or to the dispositions of their Minds," for, as Temple believes, "the true original Greatness of any Kingdom or Nation, may be accounted by the number of strong and able Bodies of their Native Subjects. This is the Natural Strength of Governments, all the rest is Art, Discipline, or Institution" (230). Another important element of the conquering spirit is "fearlessness of Mind, whether it be occasioned by the Temper of the Climate, or Race, of which Men are born, or by

Custom, which inures Men to be insensible of Danger, or be Passions or Opinions that are raised in them; for they may all have the same Effect" (230). The basis of all conquest

consists first in the choice of the strongest, ablest, and hardiest Bodies of Men: Next in the exactness of Discipline, by which they are inured to Labour and Dangers, and to fear their Commanders more than their Enemies: And lastly, in the Spirit given them by Love of their Country or their Prince, by Impressions of Honour or Religion, to render them fearless of Death and so incapable, or at least very difficult, to receive any Fright, or break thereby into Disorder. (231)

But, in the end, Temple reaffirms his earlier statement that conquest "must be confessed to hold but the second Rank in the Pretensions to Heroick Virtue, and that the first has been allowed to the wise Institution of just Orders and Laws, which frame safe and happy Governments in the World." Thus Moses is greater than Joshua; for "if, among the Ancients some Men have been esteemed Heroes, by the brave Atchievements of great Conquests and Victories; it has been, by the wise Institution of Laws and Governments, that others have been honoured and adored as Gods" (232).

Temple's survey of the four empires reinforces, therefore, his thesis that great nations are founded, shaped, and given lasting strength by men who possess heroic virtue, and who have a nobility and a magnitude of mind and character that stimulate the establishment of civilization and the conquest of nations. Thus Confucius, Mango Copac, Odin, and Mahomet clearly prove the presence of such a quality in various parts of the ancient world, not in Greece and Rome alone. Such a theory supports his cyclical hypothesis and also casts doubt upon the idea of progress which Temple so deeply distrusted.

IV *The Circle of History*

As a practicing historian, Temple produced a substantial body of literature. In the *Memoirs,* he reviews the day-to-day workings of his diplomatic career; but, in *An Introduction to the History of England* and *Of Heroick Virtue,* he views history from a somewhat more detached viewpoint. The history of early England may be a propaganda piece, but the essay on heroic virtue serves as an effective antidote to the idea of progress then being advanced. Greatness or perfection is not immortal among civilizations; they rise, flourish, and decline in various parts of the earth, leaving behind them some vestiges of their greatness for future generations to admire.

Temple's treatment of historical fact is sometimes open to question. Errors of fact and interpretation can easily be found, and various critics have attacked Temple for them. But, in light of seventeenth-century historiography, he comes off as well as, or better than, many of his contemporaries. He drew upon his many sources, evaluated them as best he could, found ample evidence for his theories, and drew his conclusions.

CHAPTER 5

Religion and Philosophy

NEXT to his role in the ancients-moderns controversy, Temple is probably best known in literary history for his essay *Upon the Gardens of Epicurus,* which was written in 1685 and published in 1690. Because of this essay, he has gained a reputation as an Epicurean, in the better sense of the word; but such an epithet is overly simple, for the master of Moor Park was also a devout Anglican who saw no conflict between his allegiance to the Church of England and his espousal of the Epicurean ethic of pleasure. Certainly, he was attracted to aspects of Epicureanism; but, like so many of his contemporaries, he found himself involved with the eternal questions regarding man and his place in the universe. In his work there is a rather substantial amount of writing which may be classified as philosophical or religious. Although he was not a systematic philosopher, his essays contain strains of various religious and philosophic elements: (1) a rather tolerant Anglicanism, (2) a skepticism toward science and rationalism, and (3) a neo-Epicureanism.

I Religion

Temple's religious position was orthodox enough. The few references to religion in his works and the comments of his sister, Lady Martha Giffard, indicate clearly that he subscribed to the major doctrines of the Anglican Church and that he was tolerant toward other faiths, even Catholicism. In her biographical sketch of her brother Lady Giffard reports that his religion was orthodox, though somewhat tinted by a mild skepticism: "His Religion was yt of the church of England he was borne & bred in, & thought nobody ought to change since it must require more time & pains then ones life can furnish to make a true judgement of that which interest & folly were commonly the motives too." [1]

Two other bits of evidence confirm Temple's essentially Christian attitude toward life. One is the "Family Prayer" written probably between 1655 and 1665, a prayer orthodox though somewhat latitudinarian in its theology. Too lengthy to be quoted in its entirety here,[2] excerpts will show how deeply Temple was immersed in the Christian tradition. He addresses God as "eternal in thy being, wonderful in thy works, but most of all in thy mercies," and thanks Him "that when we were lost by that covenant of works, thou gavest thy Son to satisfy our disobedience, and by virtue of his blood hast raised us up again to the hopes of immortal life and glory." [3] He recalls that we daily sin against God by "all our unbelief, our impenitence, and our daily transgressions"; and he admits that the Lord may therefore "justly enter into judgement against us, and close our eyes in everlasting darkness, and fill our mouths with lamentations and woes, instead of the prayers and praises we are offering up to thee." [4] The rest of the prayer continues in much the same tone: confession, repentance, a plea for forgiveness, a resolution toward a better life, and petitions for blessings of mind, spirit, and body.[5] This prayer is deeply and tolerantly Christian in its tone, its language, and its theology. In its humility and submissiveness, in its reverence and in its acknowledgment of God's grace and blessings—most important of which are Christ's mediation and propitiation—there is nothing to which an English Catholic, Anglican, or Dissenter of the seventeenth century could not easily assent.

Many of the ideas expressed in this prayer are repeated or implied in his letter of January 29, 1674, to the Countess of Essex. Having recently lost her only daughter, the Countess had not yet recovered from her grief. Temple writes to her in an admonitory spirit, and his Christian philosophy is evident throughout. He reminds her of their close friendship and warns that for her to throw away her health or her life "all by a desperate Melancholy, upon an Accident past Remedy, and to which all Mortal Race is perpetually subject" is unchristian and incompatible with the noble spirit of "so great a Person as your Ladyship appears to the World in all other Lights" (*Works*, I, 128). He tells her that there is "no Duty in Religion more generally agreed on, nor more justly required by God Almighty, than a perfect Submission to his Will in all things," and that nothing pleases God more than "being satisfied with all he gives, and contented with all he takes away." Her life, he recalls, had been relatively fortunate and serene in comparison with the lives of those who "die without Name or Children"; and he suggests that she fall upon her knees in thanksgiving for God's blessings upon her (128–29). The same theme dominates the next several pages: man can overcome grief and doubt only through unquestioning resignation to the ways of God (129–33). Commonplace as these sentiments may seem, they are certainly more than "the usual banalities about the duties of submission" that one critic has called them.[6] They are thoroughly Christian and characteristic of Temple's humanity and sympathy.

The tolerance of Temple's religion found earlier in his *Observations upon the United Provinces* and in one of his early essays is continued in *An Essay upon the Ancient and Modern Learning* (1690), in which he says that religious quarrels have not only drained Europe's lifeblood but also greatly impeded the progress of learning:

The endless Disputes and litigious Quarrels upon all these Subjects, favoured and incouraged by the Interests of the several Princes ingaged in them, either took up wholly, or generally imployed the Thoughts, the Studies, the Applications, the Endeavours of all or most of the finest Wits, the deepest Scholars, and the most learned Writers that the Age produced. Many Excellent Spirits, and the most Penetrating *Genii*, that might have made admirable Progresses and Advances in many other Sciences, were sunk and overwhelmed in the Abyss of Disputes about Matters of Religion, without ever turning their Looks or Thoughts any other way. (*Works*, I, 167)

And in *Of Poetry* (1690) he points out how the religious struggles of seventeenth-century England have resulted in intellectual chaos; there is much religious zeal, but even more knavery as the sects clash blindly and stupidly (*Works*, I, 248). Temple's tolerance was not, however, extended only to Christian sects. In *Of Heroic Virtue* (1690), he shows his respect for the strict morality of Mohammedanism (*Works*, I, 221–22); and he condemns the religion of the ancient Chinese as being "gross and sottish Idolatry," though admitting that the more learned among them worshiped the "Spirit of the World" without recourse to idols, priests, and temples (205).

Thus it appears that his Christian position reflects the *via media* of seventeenth-century Anglicanism between the extremes of Catholicism and Dissent. Unless other but now unknown evidence is forthcoming, his devotion to Christianity cannot be questioned. Secure in his own convictions, and looking with benevolent toleration and at times amusement on the religious beliefs and practices of other persons and other nations, he felt strongly that religion was a matter of individual conscience so long as its expression and practice did not endanger the commonweal. Like Swift and innumerable other Englishmen after 1660, he sought the religious settlement which would best suit the temperament of the greatest number of people.

II   Upon the Gardens of Epicurus

His Anglicanism, however, did not prevent him from being attracted to the teachings of Epicurus, especially those which taught an ethic based on mental serenity and bodily ease. This moderate Epicureanism finds its fullest expression in the essay *Upon the Gardens of Epicurus* (1690). The discussion of Epicurus and his philosophy is, certainly, secondary to the theme of gardening; but it is important if for no other reason than its prominent place in Temple's philosophy.

By nature a skeptic, Temple doubts, at the beginning of the essay, that natural philosophy (or science, as we call it) offers man any hope of finding happiness: "I know no End it can have, but that of either busying a Man's Brains to no purpose, or satisfying the Vanity so natural to most Men of distinguishing themselves, by some way or other, from those that seem their Equals in Birth, and the common Advantages of it" (*Works*, I, 172). As far as Temple is concerned, the only benefits derived from science are those of mathematics; and he cites Solomon, Socrates, and Marcus Aurelius as three ancient authorities who distrusted natural philosophy (172).

If natural philosophy is not sufficient to bring man happiness, what is? Examining ancient philosophy and finding that all of the philosophers concluded that "Happiness was the chief Good, and ought to be the ultimate End of Man; that as this was the End of Wisdom, so Wisdom was the way to Happiness," he asks, therefore, what is the nature of happiness? (173).

Earlier in this essay Temple makes a point which he had previously made elsewhere:[7] man is distinguished from the rest of creation by reason, a faculty which works both to his well-being and his harm:

'Tis this furnishes us with such Variety of Passions, and consequently of Wants and Desires, that none other feels; and these followed by infinite Designs and endless Pursuits, and improved by that Restlessness of Thought which is natural to most Men, give him a Condition of Life suitable to that of His Birth; so that as He alone is born Crying, he lives Complaining, and dies Disappointed. (170)

Man is torn between reason and passion, and, as he asserts in the *Heads Designed for an Essay upon the Different Conditions of Life and Fortune,* the chief distinction among men is "whether a Man governs his Passions, or his Passions him" (*Works,* I, 307).

Some men may divert their passions through business, sport, or other pleasures. Recreation will never satisfy man for long; and, though he may turn to business, never "growing too old for the Thoughts and Desires of increasing his Wealth and Fortunes, either for Himself, his Friends, or his Posterity" (170), wiser men, therefore, want more than riches; they seek a more certain road to the good life by "endeavouring to subdue, or at least to temper their Passions and reduce their Appetites to what Nature seems only to ask and to need" (172).

Temple thus turns to moral philosophy and shows that the ancient Stoics believed that happiness lay in virtue, whereas the Epicureans thought it could be found in pleasure. But the issue was somewhat confused, for the "most reasonable of the Stoicks made the Pleasure of Virtue to be the greatest Happiness; and the best of the *Epicureans* made the greatest Pleasure to consist in Virtue." But both agreed, says Temple, that

the greatest Temper, if not the total subduing of Passion, and exercise of Reason, to be the State of the greatest Felicity: To live without Desires or Fears, or those Perturbations of Mind and Thought, which Passions raise: To place true Riches in wanting little, rather than in possessing much; and true Pleasure in Temperance, rather than in satisfying the Senses; To live with Indifference to the common Enjoyments and Accidents of Life, and with Constancy upon the greatest Blows of Fate or of Chance; not to disturb our Minds with sad Reflections upon what is past, nor with anxious Cares or raving Hopes about what is to come; neither to disquiet Life with Fears of Death, nor Death with the Desires of Life; but in both, and in all things else, to follow Nature, seem to be the Precepts most agreed among them. (173)

The Stoics emphasized tranquility of mind, using reason to "allay those Disorders which it self had raised, to cure its own Wounds," and thought him a wise man who lived "not only without any sort of Passion, but without any Sense of Pain, as well as Pleasure," an existence which Temple dismisses as contrary to both "common Nature and common Sense" (173).[8]

On the other hand, Temple finds the Epicurean philosophy much more appealing because it places man's happiness not only in "Tranquility of Mind" but also in "Indolence of Body." Temple, of course, uses "indolence" in the seventeenth-century sense of "freedom from pain."[9] Therefore, he cannot understand why later ages have so viciously denigrated Epicurus—a man renowned in antiquity for his "Admirable Wit, Felicity of Expression, Excellence of Nature, Sweetness of Conversation, Temperance of Life, and Constancy of Death"—unless the attack was motivated by the jealousy of the Stoics, the overemphasis on sensual pleasure by some of his disciples, and the excessive piety of the early Christians. But Temple feels that Epicurus needs no apologist; his illustrious followers in later ages have spoken eloquently in his favor: Caesar, Atticus, Mecaenas, Lucretius, Vergil, and Horace (173–74).

Before Temple passes on to a discussion of gardens which involves most of the remainder of the essay, he describes Epicurus in terms reminiscent of his own retirement at Sheen and Moor Park after his frustrating years in the service of the King:

Epicurus passed his Life wholly in his Garden; there he Studied, there he Exercised, there he Taught his Philosophy; and indeed, no other sort of Abode seems to contribute so much, to both the Tranquility of Mind, and Indolence of Body, which he made his Chief Ends. The Sweetness of Air, the Pleasantness of Smells, the Verdure of Plants, the Cleanness and Lightness of Food, the Exercises of Working or Walking; but above all, the Exemption from Cares and Solicitude, seem equally to favour and improve both Contemplation and Health, the Enjoyment of Sense and Imagination, and thereby the Quiet and Ease both of the Body and Mind. (175)

This concept of Epicurean pleasure anticipates Temple's statement at the end of *An Essay upon the Ancient and Modern Learning*, where he says that "among so many things as are by Men possessed or pursued in the Course of their Lives, all the rest are Bawbles, besides Old Wood to Burn, Old Wine to Drink, Old Friends to Converse with, and Old Books to Read" (169). And it describes rather well Temple's own practice, as characterized by Lady Giffard.[10] The description made in 1694 of Temple and his estate at Moor Park by the young Swiss, Béat de Muralt, published in his *Lettres sur les Anglais* (1725), also reflects Temple's attitude toward life:

> It was in his house that I saw the ideal of a pleasant retreat; far enough from the town to be protected from visits, the air wholesome, the soil good, the view limited but pretty, a little stream which runs rear making the only sound to be heard; the house small, convenient, and appropriately furnished; the garden in proportion to the house, and cultivated by the master himself. He is free from business, and to all appearances free from ambition; he has few servants, and some sensible people for company, one of the greatest pleasures of the country for anyone lucky enough to have it. I saw also the result of this: I saw Monsieur Temple healthy and gay; and though he is gouty and getting on in years, he tired me in walking, and except for the rain which interrupted us would, I believe, have forced me to ask for quarter.[11]

Temple's comments on Epicurus in this essay are the extent of his wanderings in the tangles of Epicurean philosophy. Concerned only with the ideal of pleasure as the end of life, an ideal to be reached through tranquility of mind and soul, he says nothing at all about the Epicurean doctrines of the mortality of the soul, the impersonality of the divinity, the empirical test of truth, the atomic structure of matter, or the functions of chance and natural law in ruling the world. In other words, if Temple read his Epicurus and Lucretius well, he selected only that idea—the wisdom of the pleasurable life—which he felt compatible with his own Christian faith; and, like Walter Charleton, John Evelyn, and John Dryden, as well as others of his contemporaries, he did not feel that he was denying his religion in so doing.

Thomas F. Mayo has traced the rise and decline of a neo-Epicurean school in England in which a number of English intellectuals attempted to construct "a compromise between Christianity and Epicureanism; . . . a Christian Epicureanism." [12] Beginning about 1650 and largely through the work of Walter Charleton, John Evelyn, Thomas Creech, Ferrand Spence,

Dryden, St. Evremond, and Temple, English neo-Epicureanism reached its zenith about 1685.[13] Although its influence was particularly strong in Restoration comedy and in the poetry of Edmund Waller, the Earl of Rochester, and Abraham Cowley,[14] the movement's decline was just as rapid as its rise. An alliance of the Cartesians, the Cambridge Platonists, and the Anglican clergy, together with the aid of such writers as Sir Thomas Blount, Richard Bentley, Sir Richard Blackmore, Joseph Addison, Dr. John Arbuthnot, Pope, Swift, Matthew Prior, Francis Atterbury, and William King, was effective in striking the deathblow. By 1725 Epicureanism was dead in England.[15]

For Temple, the Epicurean ethic was a compromise in the conflict between reason and emotion. Unable to place his faith in the efforts and aims of the natural philosophers and unwilling to subordinate his own sensual inclinations to a Stoic philosophy, he found his *summum bonum* in Epicurus' ideal of moderate and refined pleasure.[16]

Although his comments on gardening are perhaps less interesting than those on Epicurus, they nevertheless show something of Temple's cultural cosmopolitanism and his broad interests. He traces the history of gardens from Eden to Rome, finding them "to have born the most Ancient and most General of and Sorts of Possession among Mankind, and to have preceded those of Corn or of Cattel, as yielding the easier, the pleasanter, and more natural Food" (*Works*, I, 175–76).

Moving on to a discussion of gardening in northern Europe, he shows that the difference between the gardens of the North and those of the South are due, like the variations in humanity, to "the different Nature of Climates, Soils or Situations, and from the Necessities or Industry they impose" (180). Thus the methods of English gardening are dictated by soil and climate. The remainder of the essay is devoted to directions for the proper arrangement and care of an English garden. His preference is for "either a Square or an Oblong, and either upon a Flat or a Descent; they have all their Beauties, but the best I esteem an Oblong upon a Descent. The Beauty, the Air, the View makes Amends for the Expence, which is very great in finishing and supporting the Terras-Talks, in levelling the Parterres, and in the Stone-Stairs that are necessary from one to the other" (185). The best garden he had ever seen was at Moor Park in Hertfordshire, the home of Sir Richard Franklin, where he and Dorothy had spent their honeymoon, from which he borrowed the name for his own estate in Surrey, and which he describes in detail (185–86).

Temple, however, does not believe that his own preference is necessarily the best arrangement for other people. The "regular" form most appeals to him, but "there may be other Forms wholly irregular, that may, for ought I know, have more beauty than any of the other"—and such a type may be the Chinese garden (186). Toward the end of the essay he confesses that his gardens have given him a large measure of serenity and happiness:

> For my own Part, as the Country Life, and this Part of it more particularly, were the Inclination of my Youth it self, so they are the Pleasure of my Age; and I can truly say, that among many great Employments that have fallen to my Share, I have never asked or sought for any one of them, but often endeavoured to escape from them, into the Ease and Freedom of a private Scene, where a Man may go his own Way and his own Pace, in the common Paths or Circles of Life. (188)

What best helps man to grow old gracefully and without care: honor, wealth, or a "private Path of stealing Life?" (188–89). Temple had long ago found his answer: "though among the Follies of my Life, Building and Planting have not been the least, and have cost me more than I have the Confidence to own; yet they have been fully recompenced by the Sweetness and Satisfaction of this Retreat, where, since my Resolution taken of never entring again into any publick Employments, I have passed five Years without ever going once to Town" (189). Like Epicurus, he could find tranquility of mind and ease of body in his garden.

The essay has its place in the extensive garden literature of the seventeenth century, in which such diverse personalities as Sir Francis Bacon, Sir Thomas Browne, Andrew Marvell, John Evelyn, Abraham Cowley, Sir Hugh Plat, Leonard Meager, and John Parkinson, among others, wrote essays, poems, or treatises on gardens and gardening. Temple's is certainly one of the best, for its transcends the more prosaic matters of the mechanics of planting and cultivation.

III   *Essays on Health*

The essays *Of Health and Long Life,* written in the early 1680's and published in 1701, and *Upon the Cure of the Gout by Moxa* (published 1679) further illustrate Temple's distrust of science and his healthy and refined Epicurean ethic. In both essays he expresses his fear of physicians and their cures, and shows that he himself was not without a degree of experimental curiosity.

The essay on health and long life is admittedly didactic, as Temple tells us at the beginning: "I can truly say, that of all the Paper I have blotted, which has been a great deal in my Time, I have never written any thing for the Publick without the Intention of some publick Good" (*Works,* I, 272). Having announced this intention, he recounts an incident from early life by way of leading into his topic:

> When I was young, and in some idle Company, it was proposed that every one should tell what their three Wishes should be, if they were sure to be granted: Some were very pleasant, and some very extravagant; mine were Health, and Peace, and fair Weather; which, though out of the way among young Men, yet perhaps might pass well enough among old: They are all of a Strain, for Health in the Body is like Peace in the State and Serenity in the Air. (273)

For Temple, there can be little pleasure in life without good health; health "is the Soul that animates all Enjoyments of Life, which fade and are tasteless, if not dead, without it": wine, sex, wealth, music, honor, and palaces. Ill health "loses not only the Enjoyments of Fortune, but the Pleasures of Sense, and even of Imagination, and hinders the common Operations both of Body and Mind from being easy and free" (273).

Temple then embarks upon a survey of "the Examples or Instances we meet with of Health and long Life . . . and the Places, and Customs, and the Conditions of those who enjoyed them in any Degree extraordinary; from whence we may best guess at the Causes, and make the truest Conclusions" (274). Consistent with his never-failing interest in diverse civilizations, he examines the health practices of the biblical patriarchs, the Brahmans, and the Brazilians; notes their longevity; and concludes that for these people the common Ingredients of Health and long Life (where Births are not impair'd from the Conception by any derived Infirmities of the Race they come from) are, great Temperance, open Air, easy Labour, little Care, Simplicity of Diet, rather Fruits and Plants than Flesh, which easier corrupts; and Water, which preserves the radical Moisture, without too much increasing the radical Heat: Whereas Sickness, Decay, and Death proceed commonly from the one preying too fast upon the other, and at length wholly extinguishing it. (275)

He then speculates about the influence of climate on health and longevity; the Northern regions seem to produce shorter lives through excessive eating, though the English seem to live longer than other Northern Europeans. He cites several examples of Englishmen living to upwards of a hundred years, but he is unable to suggest any obvious reason for this except, perhaps, the liberty of the English people (275–78).

Noting that illness is the logical result of luxury and extravagance in living, he proceeds to outline the history of medicine from the Greeks to his own time, but not without stopping to disparage Harvey's theory of blood circulation:

Doctor *Harvey* gave the first Credit, if not Rise, to the Opinion about the Circulation of the Blood, which was expected to bring in great and general Innovations into the whole Practice of Physick; but has had no such Effect. Whether the Opinion has not had the Luck to be so well believed as proved: Sense and Experience having not well agreed with Reason and Speculation: Or, whether the Scheme has not been pursued so far, as to draw it into Practice: Or, whether it be too fine to be capable of it, like some Propositions in the Mathematicks, how true and demonstrative soever, I will not pretend to determine. (280)

But Temple does not join Montaigne and others in denigrating physicians for their continually changing theories; after all, only when consistency becomes a virtue of theologians, lawyers, or politicians can it also be expected of doctors. Many of the defects in medicine are the results of the heavy emphasis "upon Method, and so little upon Medicine," a flaw which might be repaired by a registry of effective remedies in the Royal College of Physicians. If men had improved and maintained their medical knowledge as carefully as they had their property, the state of medicine might be much better (281). After tracing the history of various medical treatments, he follows the history of fads in both diseases and remedies. The most common is hypochondria, for which the doctors are hard-pressed to prescribe cures lest their patients turn to others who claim more skill and care in diagnosis and prescription, "which neither they or their Patients find any Effect of, besides some Gains to one, and Amusement to the other" (283).[17]

Temple points out that physicians rely too much on bleeding, vomiting, and purgation even though they disagree among themselves as to the proper occasions for such treatments. He recalls his own unpleasant experience:

I remember three in my Life and Observation who were as downright killed with Vomits as they could have been with Daggers; and I can say for my self, upon an Accident very near Mortal, when I was young, that sending for the two best Physicians of the Town, the first prescribed me a Vomit, and immediately sent it me: I had the Grace or Sense to refuse it till the other came, who told me if I had taken it I could not have lived Half an Hour. (283)[18]

Thus, for his own good health he would rather trust to "God Almighty, to Nature, to Temperance or Abstinence, and the Use of common Remedies" and herbs such as sage, rue, alehoof, garlic, and elder (284).

At the end of the essay, however, he gives physicians some slight praise and quotes from the Apocrypha's Ecclesiasticus 6:16: "In all Diseases of Body or Mind, 'tis happy to have an able Physician for a Friend, or a discreet Friend for a Physician; which is so great a Blessing, that the Wise Man will have it proceed only from God, where he says, *A Faithful Friend is the Medicine of Life, and he that fears the Lord shall find him*" (289). Good health, for Temple, is essential to the achievement of "Tranquility of Mind, and Indolence of Body."

We see another aspect of Temple's attitude toward medicine in his *Upon the Cure of the Gout by Moxa* (1679), which contains an amusing episode in which he becomes an amateur medical virtuoso. The piece is prefaced by a letter, dated at Nimeguen June 18, 1677, to his friend, Monsieur Zulichem, who had originally suggested the remedy. Having experienced a sharp pain in his right foot, but thinking it a strain incurred at tennis, he went to

bed. After several days the foot began to swell, and everyone recognized the symptoms of gout. At this point, Monsieur Zulichem
called to express his sympathy and to suggest moxa as a remedy:

He said it was a certain kind of Moss that grew in the *East-Indies;*
that their way was, whenever any Body fell into a Fit of the *Gout,* to
take a small quantity of it, and form it into a Figure broad at the bottom as a Two-Pence, and pointed at top; to set the bottom exactly
upon the place where the violence of the Pain was fixed; then with a
small round perfumed match . . . to give Fire to the top of the Moss;
which burning down by degrees, came at length to the Skin, and burnt
it till the Moss was consumed to Ashes: That many times the first
burning would remove the Pain; if not, it was to be renewed a second,
third, and fourth time, till it went away, and till the Person found he
could set his Foot boldly to the Ground and walk. (*Works,* I, 138)

Resolved to try the treatment, he did so three times, after the third
application placing a bit of garlic on the burned area. A day later
he opened the bandage, found a blister, and drained it. The blister reappeared for three days, but finally dried up into a sore
which disappeared in about a week. The swelling gradually declined, but it did not completely disappear for six weeks (140–
41). Elated by his success, Temple recommended it to Monsieur
Serinchamps, a representative of the Duke of Lorraine. The
man tried it, but not without loud remonstrance: "He suffer'd it;
but after his pleasant way roared out, and swore at me all the
while it was burning, and asked if I took him for a Sorcerer, that I
sent to burn him alive? Yet with all this, the Pain went away upon
it, and returned no more to the same Place" (141). At about the
same time one of Temple's maids was suffering from a toothache
so severe that she could not sleep. He applied the burning moxa to
the skin above her carotid artery, and the pain disappeared (142).

   Temple soon had a bright opportunity to establish a small medical reputation when Zulichem later invited him, on behalf of the
scientists at Gresham College, to publish the results of his experiments with the moxa. But he declined, excusing himself for reasons of business and an insufficient number of experiments to
check the accuracy of his observations: "One or two tryals can
pretend to make no Rule, no more than one Swallow a Summer;
and so before I told my Story to more than my Friends, I had a
mind to make more Tryals my self, or see them made by other

People as wise as I had been" (142). Thus ended Temple's one recorded attempt to play the part of the amateur scientist. As much as he might disparage the efforts of the virtuosi, he himself could not resist the temptation to experiment.

IV *The Christian Epicurean*

Made up of such diverse elements an Anglican orthodoxy, neo-Epicureanism, and skepticism, Temple's philosophy appears to be a potpourri which he drew together over the years. Inconsistent as it may be, it nevertheless provided a workable way of life for him, even though it could bring Gilbert Burnet to accuse him of infidelity. Burnet, in his *History of His Own Times* (1724–1734), says, "At least he [Temple] thought religion was fit only for the mob. He was a corrupter of all that came near him. And he delivered himself up wholly to study, ease, and pleasure." [19] Patently false as the charge was to all who knew Temple, Swift nevertheless made an appropriate marginal annotation in his own copy: "Sir William Temple was a man of virtue, to which Burnet was a stranger." [20]

Temple felt it his right to act, think, and speak as he pleased. And, as he looked at men and the world around him, he saw that, in the conflict between reason and passion which every man must experience, there were no completely sufficient and satisfactory solutions either in the otherworldliness of Christianity or in the abstract speculations and seemingly pointless experiments of the scientists. These, especially religion, might have their value; but man's happiness in this life could be assured only by the Epicurean ideal of the moderate and temperate life of pleasure—a life which would insure "Tranquility of Mind" and "Indolence of Body."

CHAPTER 6

Literature and Criticism

A S HIS later experiences with Wotton and Bentley were to prove, Temple was not the favorite of critics; and his own attitude toward critics is expressed in *Some Thoughts upon Reviewing the Essay of the Ancient and Modern Learning:* he thinks them but "Brokers, who having no Stock of their own, set up and trade with that of other Men; buying here, and selling there, and commonly abusing both Sides, to make out a little paultry Gain, either of Money or of Credit, for themselves, and care not at whose Cost" (*Works,* I, 299). But he himself did not hesitate to express his opinions on literature, and it is as a critic of poetry that Temple is often read and remembered today.

The largest body of Temple's criticism of literature is found in his essay *Of Poetry* (published 1690), but random comments may also be found in the other essays. He was also an amateur poet, and there survives a small volume entitled *Poems by Sir W. T.* (privately printed, no date), which contains translations from Horace and Vergil and several original poems.

I Criticism

With the essays *Upon the Ancient and Modern Learning* and *Upon the Gardens of Epicurus, Of Poetry* forms the trio of Temple's best-known works. Although his *Of Poetry* is somewhat conventional in manner and borrows from varied sources in criticism, travel, history, and philosophy, it is one of the minor monuments of English criticism; it is also, as Samuel Monk believes, Temple's most representative essay: "In no other essay do his respect for genius, his enthusiasm for the arts, his distrust of mere authority find clearer expression than in *Of Poetry.*" [1]

As the title indicates, Temple is concerned with the nature of poetry, but he deals with far more than this subject, not always satisfactorily, perhaps: the origin and history of poetry, the nature of poetic inspiration, style, versification, folklore, the relationship of poetry to prose, the romance, and satire. Woodbridge is undoubtedly right when he suggests that "no other seventeenth century essay . . . raises so many and so important questions of literary history as these." [2]

The essay begins with the observation that most men devote their time to either profit or pleasure and that by their devotion to the one or the other are called either "busy or idle Men" (*Works*, I, 233). This comment serves as an introduction to Temple's discussion of "wit" and "wisdom," the first characterizing those who seek pleasure; the second, those who seek profit. "Wit" is equivalent to the Spanish and Italian *ingenio* and the French *esprit*, but the two categories are not mutually exclusive:

Yet, according to the Opinion of those that link them together, as the Inventions of Sages and Law-givers themselves do please as well as profit those who approve and follow them; so those of Poets instruct and profit, as well as please, such as are conversant in them, and the happy Mixture of both these makes the Excellency in both those Compositions, and has given Occasion for esteeming, or at least for calling, Heroick Virtue and Poetry *Divine*. (233)

He points out that both the Greeks and the Romans conceived of the poet as divine, as a prophet and creator, as practicing the highest functions of man (233–34).

But Temple will not ascribe divine origin to poetry because for him it stems "from the greatest Excellency of natural Temper, or the greatest Race of native Genius, without exceeding the Reach of what is Human, or giving it any Approaches of Divinity" (234). The genius of poetry is explainable on natural grounds, though its powers of picture, eloquence, and music cannot be denied (234–35). Thus, "if the strength of these three mighty Powers be united in Poetry, we need not wonder that such Virtues and such Honours have been attributed to it, that it has been thought to be inspired, or has been called Divine" (235).

The real source of poetry is "a certain Noble and Vital Heat of Temper, but especially of the Brain," from which arises that "Elevation of Genius, which can never be produced by any Art or Study, by Pains or by Industry, which cannot be taught by Precepts or Examples; and therefore is agreed by all, to be the pure and free Gift of Heaven or of Nature, and to be a Fire kin-

dled out of some hidden Spark of the very first Conception"
(236). Although placing himself on the side of original genius,
Temple is sensible enough to believe that genius alone is insuffi-
cient to produce great poetry, since the poetic gift "must be
Nourished with Care, Cloathed with Exactness and Elegance,
Educated with Industry, Instructed with Art, Improved by
Application, Corrected with Severity, and Accomplished with
Labour and with Time, before it arrives at any great Perfection
or Growth" (236). The imagination, too, plays a vital role in
literary creativity, but it requires the guidance of "good Sense
and Soundness of Judgment," for "without the Forces of Wit, all
Poetry is flat and languishing; without the Succours of Judgment,
'tis wild and extravagant" (237). In short,

There must be a great Agitation of Mind to invent, a great Calm to
judge and Correct. . . . To work up this Metal into exquisite Figure,
there must be imploy'd the Fire, the Hammer, the Chizel and the
File. There must be a General Knowledge both of Nature and of Arts,
and to go the lowest that can be, there are required *Genius,* Judgment, and Application; for without this last, all the rest will not serve
turn, and none ever was a great Poet that applied himself much to any
thing else. (237)

Imagination and judgment thus complement each other in poetic
creation.

Temple goes on to define poetry as "a Just Poem," by which he
means the epic rather than the lyric or the satire. Among the epic
poets he singles out Homer and Vergil as examples of those few
authors who are "so much admired, and have almost Divinity
ascribed to them, and to their Works," and he then launches into
a lengthy comparison of the merits of the two men.[3]

Homer was, without Dispute, the most Universal *Genius* that has been
known in the World, and *Virgil* the most accomplish'd. To the first
must be allowed the most fertile Invention, the richest Vein, the most
general Knowledge, and the most lively Expression: To the last, the
noblest Idea's [*sic*], the justest Institution, the wisest Conduct, and
the choicest Elocution. To speak in the Painter's Terms, we find in the
Works of *Homer,* the most Spirit, Force and Life; in those of *Virgil,*
the best Design, the truest Proportions, and the greatest Grace; the
Colouring in both seems equal, and indeed is in both admirable.

Homer had more Fire and Rapture, *Virgil* more Light and Swiftness; or at least the Poetical Fire was more raging in one but clearer in the other, which makes the first more amazing, and the latter more agreeable. The Ore was richer in one, but in the other more refined, and better allay'd to make up excellent Work. Upon the whole, I think it must be confessed, that *Homer* was of the two, and perhaps of all others, the vastest, and sublimest, and the most wonderful *Genius*. . . . In short, these two immortal Poets must be allowed to have so much excelled in their Kinds, as to have exceeded all Comparison, to have even extinguished Emulation, and in a Manner confined true Poetry, not only to their two Languages, but to their very Persons. (237)

For every poetic genius such as Homer or Vergil who appears in a millennium, a thousand are born who have the potential to become great generals or ministers (238).

Temple turns quickly to a discussion of the "rules." Censuring the modern French critics in general for presuming to prescribe rules, he suggests that they should have been satisfied with those of Aristotle and Horace. Such fetters on the creative spirit are deadening:

The Truth is, there is something in the *Genius* of Poetry, too Libertine to be confined to so many Rules; and whoever goes about to subject it to such Constraints, loses both its Spirit and Grace, which are ever Native, and never learnt, even of the best Masters. 'Tis as if, to make excellent Honey, you should cut off the Wings of your Bees, confine them to their Hive or their Stands, and lay Flowers before them, such as you think the sweetest, and like to yield the finest Extraction; you had as good pull out their Stings, and make arrant Drones of them. They must range through Fields, as well as Gardens, chuse such Flowers as they please, and by Properties and Scents they only know and distinguish: They must work up their Cells with Admirable Art, extract their Honey with infinite Labour, and sever it from the Wax, with such Distinction and Choice, as belongs to none but themselves to perform or to judge. (238)[4]

Since the literature produced according to the rules has been of uneven quality, the real test of poetic merit is the power of poetry to stimulate the minds and hearts of its audience: "Whoever does not affect and move the same present Passions in you, that he represents in others, and at other Times, raise Images about you,

as a Conjurer is said to do Spirits, Transport you to the Places and
to the Persons he describes, cannot be judged to be a Poet, though
his Measures are never so just, his Feet never so smooth, or his
Sounds never so sweet," (239). Thus the rules are subordinate to
an original genius nurtured by training, practice, and reason. In
attacking the hidebound conception of the rules advocated by
some of his contemporaries, he runs counter to the prescriptions
of P. Rapin, Nicolas Boileau-Despreaux, and René Le Bossu, and
their apologists in England; and in upholding the value of genius
he anticipates the romantic tendencies of the later eighteenth
century.

The remainder of the essay traces the history of poetry. According to Temple, poetry was the forerunner of the alphabet in
several nations, most probably in America, Scythia, Greece, and
Germany. Furthermore, much of the early law, history, and philosophy first appeared in poetic form, especially among the Chal-
deans, the Syrians, and the Chinese. Even among the Hebrews,
the earliest literature—the Book of Job and the songs of Moses
and Deborah—was poetic in form. The purpose of early poetry
was largely mnemonic: "the true and general End was but the
Help of Memory, in preserving that of Words and of Actions,
which would otherwise have been lost, and soon vanish away,
with the transitory Passages of humane Breath and life" (240).

Briefly considering the types and topics of poetry and rapidly
surveying ancient literature to illustrate his classifications, he says
that generally the subjects have been praise, instruction, story,
love, grief, and reproach. Dramatic poetry, however, employs all
of these:

the chief End seems to have been Instruction, and under disguise of
Fables, or the Pleasure of Story to shew the Beauties and Rewards of
Virtue, the Deformities and Misfortunes, or Punishment of Vice; by
Examples of both to encourage one, and deter Men from the other;
to reform ill Custom, correct ill Manners, and moderate all violent
Passions. These are the general Subjects of both Parts, tho' Comedy
give us but the Images of common Life, and Tragedy those of the
greater and extraordinary Passions and Actions among Men. (241)

But, he admits, to treat this subject further "would be to tread so
beaten Paths, that to travel in them only raises Dust, and is nei-

ther of Pleasure nor of Use" (241). And thus he turns to a discussion of "the Declines or Decays of this great Empire of Wit."

Among the earlier changes he includes the metamorphosis from pure poetry to poetic prose which disguised "the true Beauty of its Features, and Exactness of its Shape," as seen in Aesop, the Miletian tales, Lucian, Petronius Arbiter, and Sir Philip Sidney, whom he praises as "the greatest Poet and the noblest Genius of any that have left Writings behind them, and published in ours or any other modern Language; a Person born capable not only of forming the greatest Ideas, but of leaving the noblest Examples, if the Length of his Life had been equal to the Excellence of his Wit and Virtues" (241).

The true cause of the decay of ancient poetry is to be found in the invasions of Rome by the barbarians, after which "Learning grew every Day more and more obscured by that Cloud of Ignorance, which coming from the North, and increasing with the Numbers and Successes of those barbarous People, at length overshadowed all Europe for so long together" (242). The decline of Roman influence opened the way for the emergence of a barbarian poetry which Temple calls the runic.

The discussion of runic poetry begins with his ascription of the invention of runes (from which, according to Temple, the modern word "rhymes" evolved) to Odin, the Gothic chieftain.[7] With a long poetic tradition behind them, the Goths used runes as a generic term for all poetry. The most successful of the Gothic sage-poets "were termed wise Men, the good Sense, or Learning, or useful Knowledge contained in them was called Wisdom, and the pleasant or facetious Vein among them was called Wit, which was applied to all Spirit or Race of Poetry, where it was found in any Men, and was generally pleasing to those that heard or read them." (242–43). He goes on to describe the types and techniques of the runic poetry as used in the Gothic languages as well as "that barbarous *Latin* which remained and was preserved among the Monks and Priests" (243). Subject matter was chiefly devoted to "Records of bold and martial Actions, and the Praises of valiant Men that had fought successfully or died bravely; and these Songs or Ballads were usually sung at Feasts, or in Circles of young and idle Persons, and served to inflame the Humour of War, or Slaughter, and of Spoils among them." Themes of honor or love were neglected because "honour among them consisted in Victory, and Love in Rapes and in Lust" (243).

Some of the runic poetry degenerated into the charms and incantations of the witches and wizards. From these came folklore and magic, traces of which Temple found in seventeenth-century Ireland (243–44). In this perverted state of medieval poetry, "those Shades of Ignorance that overspread all Europe for so many Ages after the Sunset of the Roman Learning and Empire together" (245).

Leaving the older poetry and turning to the Renaissance, Temple discusses the rediscovery of learning. The two classical languages caused the revival of poetry "to appear very early, tho' very unlike it self, and in Shapes as well as Cloaths, in Humour and in Spirit very different from the Ancient," its most distinguishing feature being rhyme. During the Renaissance "the Ore begun to shine in the Hands and Works of the first Refiners": Petrarch, Ronsard, and Spenser in the lyric; Ariosto and Tasso in the epic, though their attempts at Christian heroic poems were less than successful because Christianity was not as compatible to heroic treatment as was paganism. Spenser, however, attempted to moralize instead of merely narrate in the epic, but "his Moral lay so bare, that it lost the Effect; 'tis true the Pill was Gilded, but so thin, that the Colour and the Taste were too easily discovered" (245).

But these are the last achievements in epic poetry that the moderns have made, says Temple; the modern poets have "contented themselves with the Scraps, with Songs and Sonnets, with Odes and Elegies, with Satyrs and Panegyricks, and what we call Copies of Verses upon any Subjects or Occasions; wanting either Genius or Application for Nobler or more Laborious Productions, as Painters that cannot succeed in great Pieces, turn to Miniature" (245). Neither Milton nor Dante is mentioned in Temple's survey of great heroic poetry; the reasons for these omissions are probably not so clear as one scholar would have them.[8]

The moderns, in Temple's eyes, have attempted to make up for their lack of poetic subject by masking it under "conceit" and "ridicule," neither of which was much valued by the classical writers, the conceit being merely a spice to cover unwholesomeness: "an Ingredient, that gave Taste to Compositions which had little of themselves; 'twas a Sauce that gave Point to Meat that was flat, and some Life to Colours that were fading; and in short, those who could not furnish Spirit, supplied it with this Salt, which may preserve Things or Bodies that are dead; but is, for ought I know, of little use to the Living, or necessary to Meats that have much or pleasing Tastes of their own" (245–46). Thus modern poetry "would have Conceit as well as Rhyme in every Two Lines, and run through all our long Scribbles as well as the short, and the whole Body of the Poem, whatever it is: This was just as if a Building should be nothing but Ornament, or Cloaths nothing but Trimming; as if a Face should be covered over with black Patches, or a Gown with Spangles; which is all I shall say of it" (246).

The other modern aberration is "ridicule," which was encouraged by its fashion in conversation. Its father was Rabelais, "a Man of Excellent and universal Learning as well as Wit," who, though he had subjects sufficient for satire—the court, religion, education, and literature—wrote "many Things so malicious, so Smutty, and so Prophane" (246). On the other hand, Cervantes is admirable for constructing a satire without resorting to Rabelais' tone and method. Tracing the history of "ridicule" from Tassoni's *La Secchia Rapita* (1622) to Samuel Butler and Charles Cotton, he concludes that, "let the Execution be what it will, the Design, the Custom, and Example are very pernicious to Poetry, and indeed to all Virtue and good Qualities among Men, which must be disheartned, by finding how unjustly and undistinguished they fall under the Lash of Raillery, and this Vein of ridiculing the Good as well as the Ill, the Guilty and the Innocent together" (246).

Temple also decries the modern penchant for "Smoothness of Language or Stile." He attributes the strength of this fad to the influence of the French Academy founded by Cardinal Richelieu "to amuse the Wits of that Age and Country, and divert them from raking into his Politick and Ministry." Consequently, poets have recently concerned themselves with refinement of language, with some degree of success; but in England the results have been less obviously successful. Nevertheless, the true lover of poetry will not be discouraged; they will "think her a Beauty in Rags as well as in Robes" (247).

In spite of the general decline of poetry, Temple points out that dramatic poetry had flourished in Italy, France, and Spain, but

most of all in England, where the drama has "in some kind excelled both the Modern and the Ancient . . . by Force of a Vein
natural perhaps to our Country, and which with us is called Humour, a Word peculiar to our Language too, and hard to be expressed in any other." The origin of "humour" Temple finds in
Shakespeare; it has run "freely and so pleasantly ever since" (247).

This "humour" is "a Picture of particular Life, as Comedy is of
general; and tho' it represents Dispositions and Customs less common, yet they are not less natural than those that are more frequent among Men, for if Humour it self be forced, it loses all the
Grace, which has been indeed the Fault of some of our Poets most
celebrated in this kind." Thus English drama has surpassed the
ancient in characterization; whereas the classical dramatists relied heavily upon stock characters, the English have "come to
have more Originals, and more that appear what they are; we
have more Humour because every Man follows his own, and takes
a Pleasure, perhaps a Pride, to shew it" (247).

The true source of English "humour" is in the variety of English
life which in turn proceeds "from the native Plenty of our Soil, the
Unequalness of our Climate, as well as the Ease of our Government, and the Liberty of professing Opinions and Factions, which
perhaps our Neighbours may have about them, but are forced to
disguise" (247). The lack of "humour" he attributes to tyrannous
government and the resultant poverty of its people (247–48).

But the individuality of the English character arises from climate. In short, Temple says, "I have not observed among any so
much true Genius as among the *English;* no where more Sharp-
ness of Wit, more Pleasantness of Humour, more Range cf Fancy,
more Penetration of Thought or Depth of Reflection among the
better sort; no where more Goodness of Nature and of Meaning,
nor more Plainness of Sense and of Life, than among the common
sort of Country People; nor more blunt Courage and Honesty
than among our Sea-Men" (248). The weather makes Englishmen
"unequal in our Humours, inconstant in our Passions, uncertain in
our Ends, and even in our Desires," the proof of which can readily
be found in the various extravagances in English politics, society,
learning, and religion. Thus, "What Effect soever such a Composition or Medley of Humours among us may have upon our Lives or
our Government, it must needs have a good one upon our Stage,
and has given admirable Play to our comical Wits; so that, in my

Opinion, there is no Vein of that sort, either ancient or modern, which excells or equals the Humour of our Plays" (248).

The essay draws to a rapid close as Temple surveys the great men of ancient Israel, Greece, and Rome who esteemed poetry; and he praises the effects of poetry and its sister art, music:

They must be confest to be the softest and sweetest, the most general and most innocent Amusements of common Time and Life. They still find Room in the Courts of Princes, and the Cottages of Shepherds. They serve to revive and animate the dead Calm of poor or idle Lives, and to allay or divert the violent Passions and Perturbations of the greatest and busiest Men. And both these Effects are of equal use to human Life; for the Mind of Man is like the Sea, which is neither agreeable to the Beholder nor the Voyager in a Calm or in a Storm, but is so to both when a little agitated by gentle Gales; and so the Mind, when moved by soft and easy Passions and Affections. (249)

Poetry and music are therefore not trifles unworthy of serious men; instead, a dislike of these "may be thought at least an ill Sign, if not an ill Constitution." For, after all, Temple believes, "When all is done, Human Life is, at the greatest, and the best but like a froward Child, that must be play'd with and humour'd a little to keep it quiet till it falls asleep, and then the Care is over" (249).

Temple's essay on poetry is one of the more important critical documents of the seventeenth century. In his praise of original genius over the rules, in his historical appreciation of the evolution and development of poetry, in his accounting for a nation's literary achievement in terms of the character of its people and of its physical environment, and in his interest in Scandinavian literature, Temple diverges from the prevailing critical standards of his time and anticipates those of the pre-Romantics (if one may stipulate such a term) several generations later. Clara Marburg is right in saying that Temple's essay "marks a transition from the absolute manner of judging literature to a more tentative, historical approach." [9] Although the essay contains many current truisms, Temple's common sense attitude makes it a highly commendable piece of criticism.

II *Poems*

Temple's own attempts at poetry are much less fortunate than his critical essay. The small corpus of his poems is contained in a thin privately printed volume, *Poems by Sir W. T.* (no date) and in Part III of the *Miscellanea*, published in 1701 by Swift. The small book of poetry contains three translations from Vergil and four from Horace, as well as three original poems, while the poetry in the *Miscellanea* includes five of the previous poems and two more translations, one from Horace and one from Tibullus.

The dating of these poems is difficult, but the earliest of them were probably written shortly before 1660, and the later ones cannot be dated much later than 1671.[10] In any case, the dates are relatively unimportant; for the poems are clearly the occasional products of idle hours. Their private publication during Temple's lifetime or, in some cases, their posthumous printing, indicates that he probably did not regard them as part of his major literary work. The poems tell us little about Temple's attitudes toward poetry and do not in any noticeable way add to the ideas found in his essay on poetry.

The Latin translations are from Vergil, Horace, and Tibullus. In his preface to the *Miscellanea*, Part III, Swift calls them "imitations" and indicates that they were "done by the Author above Thirty Years ago. . . . *They were indeed not intended to have been made publick, till I was informed of several Copies that were got Abroad, and those very imperfect and corrupt. Therefore the Reader finds them here, only to prevent him from finding them in other Places very faulty and perhaps accompanied with many spurious Additions.*"[11] For convenience the originals of Temple's translations are: Horace, *Epistles*, I, 2 (passage); Horace, *Satires*, I, 1; Horace, *Odes*, I, 13, III, 29 and IV, 7; Vergil, last eclogue; Vergil, *Georgics*, II, 458ff., IV, 317ff.; Tibullus, IV, 2 (passage). Although these translations or paraphrases are not likely to be included in an anthology of Latin poetry, they are nevertheless competent and readable. We need only compare them with better-known translations to note Temple's ability. The subject matter is congenial to his spirit; generally he praises the simple and moderate life devoid of avarice, flattery, and overweening ambition—the type of life he himself led and advocated at other places in his works. Whether there was any conscious selection of the Latin classics, we cannot say.

On the other hand, the original poems seem to be more consciously Temple's own. The poem on the death of Katherine Philips (1631-64), "the Matchless Orinda," in iambic pentameter couplets, is of the conventional elegiac strain. The poem, "made at the Desire of My Lady Temple," begins with an ironical statement that death is not really malignant:

> Why all these looks so solemn and so sad!
> Who is that one can dye and none be glad!
> The Rich leaves Heirs, the Great makes room, the Wise
> Pleases the foolish onely when he dyes.[12]

But the Stoic pose is broken when the poet learns that the death is Orinda's, and he describes her in a series of epithets: "the glory of our Stage!/Crown of her Sex, and wonder of the age!" (11-12). Temple praises her grace of body and mind

> that taught sullen Vertue to be kind,
> Youth to be wise, Mirth to be innocent,
> Fame to be steddy, Envy to relent;
> Love to be cold, and Friendship to be warm,
> Praise to do good, and Wit to do no harm. (13-17).

He describes her as one "that was sent the World to give/The best example how to write and live!/The Queen of Poets, whoso'er's the King" (18-21).

Temple then mourns her death in the conventional lament for the early death of a talented young person:

> . . . But she was young
> And might have liv'd to tune the World, and sung
> Us all asleep that now lament her fall,
> And fate unjust, Heav'n unrelenting call.
> Alas! can any fruit grow ripe in Spring,
> And hang till Autumn? Nature gives this sting,
> To all below, whatever thrives too fast
> Decays too soon, late growths may longer last. (31-38)

Her soul is like a meteor that amazes all who see it:

> . . . first it calls
> The Neighbours onely to admire the light
> And lustre that surprize their wondring sight,
> Till kindling all, it grows a noble flame,
> Towring and spring up from whence it came;
> But e'er arrived at those azure Walls,
> The house that lodg'd it here, to ashes falls:
> Such was Orinda's Soul. (42–49)

The poem closes as the mourners, singing in elegiac strains, bring cypress (a symbol of mourning) to trade for bays (a symbol of literary honor): "And he deserves it who of all the rest/Praises and imitates *Orinda* best" (51–54).

"Upon Mrs. Philipp's Death" is the conventional poem we might expect from one whose main interests lay in history and politics. A second original poem, "Upon My Lady Giffard's Loory," is much more familiar and at ease. In slightly more than one hundred lines, he describes the death of his sister's parrot. In the first stanza he suggests that the bird, "the fair and charming *Loory*," must have been a native of Paradise. The second stanza describes the bird's body; he was so beautiful that

> Thus by fond Nature was he drest more gay
> Than Eastern Kings in all their rich array,
> Far Feather much, as well as Flow'er outvies
> In softness, silk, in colour mortal dies. (31–34)

Even more wonderful, as shown in stanza three, was his soul:

> If ever any reasonable Soul
> Harbor'd in shape of either brute or fowl,
> This was the Mansion, Metamorphosie
> Gained here the credit lost in Poetrie.
> Nor passion moving in a humane breast
> Was plainer seen, or livelier exprest.
> No wit or learning, eloquence or song,
> Acknowledg'd kindness, or complain'd of wrong
> With accents half so feeling as his notes.
>   (39–47)

Furthermore, as we discover in the next stanza, the bird was a favorite entertainer,

> Sprawling upon his back and pitching pyes,
> Twirling his head, and flurring at the flies.
> A thousand tricks and postures would he show,
> Then rise so pleas'd both with himself and you,
> That the amaz'd beholders could not say
> Whether the bird was happier, or they.
>
> (61–66)

The remaining two stanzas deal with the bird's death. Giving Lady Giffard the pastoral name of Artemesia, Temple describes her beloved parrot:

> Fed with her hands, and perched upon her head,
> From her lips water'd, nested in her bed.
> Nurst with her cares, preserved with her fears,
> And now, Alas! embalmed with her tears.
>
> (81–84)

He closes by philosophizing that life would be sweet and long should he find a man who excels his fellows as much as the parrot excelled all other birds; had Loory lived in polytheistic ages, he would have been mistaken for Mercury and would have been better worshiped than "Gods that perjur'd, Goddesses that whor'd" (106).

The poem is a fanciful one, and it owes much to Ovid's elegy for Corinna's parrot. The essayist and diplomat who studied the rise and fall of civilizations and constructed alliances could also condescend to writing light verse on the death of a family pet.

Perhaps the most personal and best of his original poetry is his "Upon the Approach of the Shore at Harwich in January 1668." "Begun under the Mast," the poem is an outpouring of Temple's patriotism as he returns to "the fairest and the happiest Earth,/ Seat of my Hopes and Pleasures, as my Birth," a nation of "good Nature," "good Cheer," "region of Valour and of Beauty too" (*Works*, I, 319). The sight of England after an unpleasant journey is understandably a welcome one:

Beaten with Journies, both of Land and Seas,
Weary'd with Care, the busy Man's Disease;
Pinch'd with the Frost, and parched with the Wind;
Giddy with rowling, and with fasting pin'd;
Spighted and vex'd that Winds, and Tides, and Sands,
Should all conspire to cross such great Commands,
As haste me home, with an Account, that brings
The Doom of Kingdoms to the best of Kings:
Yet I respire at thy reviving Sight,
Welcome as Health, and chearful as the Light.
How I forget my Anguish and my Toils,
Charm'd at th' Approach of thy delightful Soils! (319)

He then describes the beauty of the English countryside and the
security it affords its people, as contrasted with the plight of those
on the Continent "by cruel Lords enslav'd,/Ruined by Taxes, and
by Soldiers brav'd," who "Know no more Ease than just what
Sleep can give;/Have no more Heat and Courage but to live." The
English are "Safe in their Laws, and easie in their Rent,/Blest in
their King, and in their State content" (320). Temple continues
with a long apostrophe to the "Fortunate Island" and foresees a
glorious future for the nation, one in which disaster is unknown
and "Health and Plenty vye,/Which shall seem kindest to thee,
Earth or Sky" (320–21). He ends:

May'st thou feel no more Fits of factious Rage,
But all Distempers may thy *Charles* assuage,
With such a well-tun'd Concord of his State,
As none but ill, and hated Men, may hate.
And may'st thou from him endless Monarchs see,
Whom thou may'st honour, who may honour thee.
May they be *wise* and *good:* Thy happy Seat,
And Stores, will never fail to make them *Great.* (321)

Temple's praise of Charles might have been somewhat more moderate had he been able to foresee his own political disappoint-
ments and the king's treachery.

In this poem, we sense that Temple is truly himself. His relief at
returning from alien shores, his joy at seeing his country again, his
intense patriotism, and his confidence in England's future—these

notes ring true; for they are echoed in one way or another in most of his other work.

These three original poems—upon Orinda, upon Lady Giffard's parrot, and upon his return to England—show that Temple possessed a moderate poetic talent. It is both intriguing and useless to speculate whether more concentrated attention to poetic creativity might have given us another Restoration Poet.

Professor Moore Smith reprints two other poems sometimes attributed to Temple: "A Description of Mother Ludwell's Cave" and "To Mother Ludwell's Cave and Spring." [13] The authorship of these works is so uncertain that they are not to be discussed here. Moore Smith suggests that the first poem was perhaps written by Swift and the second by Lady Giffard, but the editor of Swift's poetry doubts the attribution to Swift.[14] There is no reliable evidence to suggest that Temple may have written them, and thus the matter rests.

III   *The Writer as Critic*

Temple's discussion of poetry and his own translations and poems are completely in keeping with his thought and character, for they show a mind sensitive to the tastes and attitudes of the age. Although some of his ideas in the essay on poetry are critical commonplaces of the seventeenth century, others are very much original. His dismissal of the rules, his insistence on the importance of the imagination, his interest in the poetic traditions outside those of Greece and Rome, and his drawing of parallels between poetry, painting, and music—all these are indicative of his commonsense approach to art, of his insatiable intellectual curiosity, and of his willingness to think for himself and to go against current popular notions. And even those ideas in the essay which are not original come close to exemplifying Alexander Pope's definition of wit: "What oft was thought, but ne'er so well expressed" (*Essay on Criticism*, II, 297–98).

But the essay also manifests an attitude which lies behind two of Temple's other works, the essays on ancient and modern learning: a strong distrust of the claims of superiority voiced by the modern writers such as Boccaccio, Cervantes, Rabelais, Montaigne, Sidney, and Bacon; and an apparent blindnesss to, or ignorance of, the merits of Dante and Milton.

On the other hand, Temple's poetry is less easy to judge. The translations are competent but unexciting, while the body of his original poetry is so small that one is hard-pressed to judge its merits with any degree of certainty. It does not break with the traditions of seventeenth-century verse, and it does not fore-shadow any later poetic movements. Temple was probably satis-fied with the pleasure of composition; and, since he did not intend it for a public audience, we can hardly be very critical of it.

CHAPTER 7

Ancients and Moderns

TEMPLE'S scholarship never caused him any notable difficulty before the publication of *An Essay upon the Ancient and Modern Learning* (1690). None of the few factual errors and glittering generalities in his earlier works had risen to haunt him and mar his reputation. But the essay on learning created a lasting but infamous niche for Temple in the history of English literature. The man known to his contemporaries as an urbane essayist and memoirist has been presented as a critical fool to many modern students; the charming writer of the essay on gardens and poetry is now often viewed as a gullible and uncritical dilettante.

But the matter is hardly so simple as many still believe. More than just a raising of dust clouds among the pedants, the so-called battle of the books was a consequence of the controversy initiated early in the seventeenth century when the revolution in learning under the leadership of Bacon attacked ancient authority.[1] R. F. Jones rightly says that Temple's essay was "only a revival of those attacks on the new science and the Royal Society that characterized the Restoration."[2] Until the late seventeenth century, the main issues in the debate were largely scientific and philosophical; but literature was occasionally involved tangentially. As Bacon and his followers mounted their attack on the scientific authority of Aristotle and the ancients, others came forward to defend traditional knowledge. Temple's *An Essay upon the Ancient and Modern Learning* and its sequel, *Some Thoughts upon Reviewing the Essay of Ancient and Modern Learning,* are part of this controversy and must be understood as such.

It is against the background of this intellectual quarrel that Temple's essays must be read, for to do otherwise would be unfair to him and would draw a picture badly out of perspective. The two essays on learning merit study in their own right and not merely as the literary reference points for Swift's *Battle of the Books* and *A Tale of a Tub* (both 1704).

I   An Essay upon the Ancient and Modern Learning

The ostensible occasion for the first essay was Temple's reading of Fontenelle's *Discours sur l'eglogue* and *Digression sur les anciens et les modernes* (1688). In the first work, the Frenchman had unfavorably compared the pastorals of Theocritus and Vergil to his own; in the second, he surveyed the whole field of learning and, while granting eminence to the ancients in poetry and eloquence, decided that in the sciences, as well as in some of the arts, the moderns had shown superiority over their predecessors. These ideas had earlier been anticipated in his *Nouveaux dialogues des mortes*, which Anne Burlingame describes as his "earliest and most flippant examination of ancient culture . . . one scathing fire of ridicule," [3] although she admits that his attack upon the ancients originated in his keen intellectual temper and not in malevolence: "The fact that the absurdities exposed are not the essential element of classical content, does not diminish their impressiveness. . . . The little book is, rather, a natural fruit of Fontenelle's lively mind at play upon a set of cut-and-dried concepts which lured him to examination." [4]

At the beginning of his own essay, undoubtedly irritated by the Frenchman's attitude, Temple isolates Fontenelle's two main premises and sets them up for attack:

first, as to Knowledge; that we must have more than the Ancients, because we have the advantage both of theirs and our own, which is commonly illustrated by the Similitude of a Dwarf's standing upon a Gyant's shoulders, and seeing more or farther than he. Next as to Wit or Genius, that Nature being still the same, these must be much at a Rate in all Ages, at least in the same Climates, as the Growth and Size of Plants and Animals commonly are; and if both these are allowed, they think the Cause is gained. (*Works*, I, 152)

Disagreeing vehemently, Temple devotes a major portion of his essay to analyzing and destroying these two arguments.

He first proceeds to turn the primary argument of the moderns against them by demonstrating that, just as the moderns had their ancestors in the ancients, so those had had their own intellectual predecessors. As evidence for his argument he cites the famous library at Alexandria, the lost learning of various civilizations, and the long oral tradition of learning before the use of writing. He then describes the travels of Pythagoras and the progress of learning from India to Greece and Italy (152–58).

The second modern argument is refuted by Temple's assertion that wisdom is the result of genius rather than accumulation and progress: men's abilities, he says, "grow directly out of that little grain of Intellect or good Sense, which they bring with them into the World," a gift which may be improved or impaired by education and experience, but cannot transcend its own limitations (158). Learning may even stifle a man's creativity: "Besides, who can tell, whether Learning may not even weaken Invention, in a Man that has great Advantages from Nature and Birth; whether the weight and number of so many other Mens Thoughts and Notions, may not suppress his own, or hinder the Motion and Agitation of them, from which all Invention arises; as heaping on Wood, or too many Sticks, or too close together, suppresses, and sometimes quite extinguishes a little Spark that would otherwise have grown up to a noble Flame" (158–59). In other words, as Temple turns Fontenelle's metaphor of the dwarf and giant to his own advantage, a dwarf is still a dwarf, even while he stands on the shoulders of a giant (159).

Temple has no quarrel with the modern assertion that the creative force of nature is constant, but he attacks the corollary which the moderns illogically drew from it: that genius appears in equal force in all ages. "May there not many Circumstances concur to one Production, that do not to any other, in one or many Ages?" he asks. The varying degrees of intellectual and artistic genius in different ages and places, despite the constancy of creative force, are the result of environment. Individual genius can arrive at the height of its powers only in conducive surroundings (159).

To counter the arguments of the moderns, Temple proposes his own theory of the history of civilization. Ignoring the current and popular hypothesis of nature's decay, he advocates once again a cyclical thesis: "Sciences and Arts have run their Circles, and had their Periods in the several Parts of the World: They are generally agreed, to have held their course from *East* to *West,* to have begun in *Chaldea and AEgypt,* to have been Transplanted from thence to *Greece,* from *Greece* to *Rome;* to have sunk there, and after many Ages, to have revived from those Ashes and to have sprung up again, both in *Italy* and other more *Western* Provinces of *Europe*" (159–60). He then surveys the decline of learning, equates it with the fall of Rome, and traces the low state of learning in the Middle Ages (160–61).

Although Temple concedes the great progress made during the Renaissance, he denies that this advance in knowledge proves the superiority of the moderns. After all,

If a Strong and Vigorous Man at thirty Years old should fall into a Consumption, and so draw on till Fifty in the extreamest Weakness and Infirmity; after that, should begin to recover Health till sixty, so as to be again as strong as Men usually are at that Age: It might perhaps truly be said in that case, that he had grown more in Strength that last ten Years than any others of his Life; but not that he was grown to more Strength and Vigour, than he had at thirty Years old. (161)

The "progress" of the moderns must be measured, therefore, against the learning of the ancients rather than that of the Middle Ages.

Then, by asking in what sciences the moderns pretend to excellence, Temple debunks the modern claims: "I know of no New Philosophers, that have made Entries upon that Noble Stage for fifteen hundred Years past, unless *Des Cartes* and *Hobbs* should pretend to it; of whom I shall make no Critick here, but only say, That by what appears of Learned Mens Opinions in this Age they have by no means eclipsed the Lustre of *Plato, Aristotle, Epicurus,* or others of the Ancients" (162). The Copernican system and Harvey's theory of the circulation of the blood may not even be modern discoveries, but only "derived from old Fountains." Even if true, they have "made no Change in the Conclusions of *Astronomy,* nor in the Practice of Physick, and so have been of little Use to the World, though perhaps of much Honour to the Authors" (162).

And in the same manner Temple discusses other areas of learning. Music and poetry have degenerated into mere fiddling and rhyming; magic (defined by Temple as "some excelling Knowledge of Nature, and the various Powers and Qualities in its several

Productions, and the Application of certain Agents to certain Patients, which by Force of some peculiar Qualities produce Effects very different from what fall under vulgar Observation or Comprehension") has become powerless. Architecture has produced nothing comparable to the wonders of the ancients; navigation, though aided by the invention of the lodestone, is still crude, and modern geography consequently suffers; painting and sculpture have made "a great but short Flight" (162–64). In a short digression on man's middle state ("We are born to grovel upon the Earth, and we would fain sore up to the Skies"), he attacks the presumptuous intellectual pride of the modern:

His own Reason is the certain Measure of Truth, his own Knowledge, of what is possible in Nature though his Mind and his Thoughts change every Seven Years, as well as his Strength and his Features; nay, though his Opinions change every Week or every Day, yet he is sure, or at least confident, that his present Thoughts and Conclusions are just and true, and cannot be deceived; and, among all the Miseries, to which Mankind is born and subjected in the whole Course of his Life, he has this one Felicity to comfort and support him, that in all Ages, in all Things, every Man is always in the right. A Boy of Fifteen is wiser than his Father at Forty, and meanest Subject than his Prince or Governours; and the Modern Scholars, because they have for a Hundred Years past learned their Lesson pretty well, are much more knowing than the Ancients their Masters. (164–65)

A quick comparative survey of the works of the ancients and moderns in science, philosophy, history, and poetry shows the superiority of the ancients:

Have the Studies, the Writings, the Productions of *Gresham* College, or the late Academies of *Paris,* outshined or eclipsed the *Lycaeum* of *Plato,* the *Academy* of *Aristotle,* the *Stoa* of *Zeno,* the *Garden* of *Epicurus?* Has *Harvey* out-done *Hippocrates,* or *Wilkins, Archimedes?* Are *D'Avila's* and *Strada's* Histories beyond those of *Herodotus* and *Livy?* Are *Sleyden's* Commentaries beyond those of *Caesar?* the Flights of *Boileau* above those of *Virgil?* If all this must be allowed, I will then yield *Gondibert* to have excelled *Homer,* as is pretended; and the Modern *French* Poetry, all that of the Ancients. And yet, I think, it may be as reasonably said, that the Plays in *Moor-Fields* are beyond the *Olympick* Games; a *Welsh* or *Irish* Harp excels those of *Orpheus*

and *Arion;* the Pyramid in *London* those of *Memphis;* and the *French*
Conquests in *Flanders* are greater than those of *Alexander* and *Caesar*,
as their Operas and Panegyricks would make us believe. (165)

At times Temple is not at all unwilling to stack his evidence so as
to embarrass the moderns.

Temple, however, excludes prose from his extended discussion;
for modern prose works, he says, will not live long, because the
languages are constantly changing "as to be hardly known for the
same . . . , so as they can no more last like the Ancients, than
excellent Carvings in Wood, like those in Marble or Brass" (165).
For this reason, Latin and Greek are preferable to their modern
descendants; and had Temple been satisfied with these denigrating comments about modern languages he would have avoided disaster. But, in surveying the prose of the ancients, he praises Aesop
and Phalaris: "The two most Ancient, that I know of in Prose,
among those we call Profane Authors, are *AEsop's Fables*, and
Phalaris's Epistles, both living near the same time. . . . As the
first has been agreed by all Ages since, for the greatest Master in
his kind, and all others of that Sort have been but Imitations of his
Original; so I think the Epistles of *Phalaris* to have more Race,
more Spirit, more Force of Wit and Genius than any others I have
ever seen, either Ancient or Modern" (166). With this claim he
bared himself to the damaging criticism which William Wotton
and Richard Bentley later directed at him.

After praising the ancient prose writers, Temple moves on to
their modern counterparts, among whom he admires Boccaccio,
Machiavelli, Paolo Sarpi, Cervantes, Guevara, Rabelais, Montaigne, Sidney, Bacon, John Selden, Voiture, Rochefoucauld, and
Bussy de Rabutin (166–67). For, as much as he might revere the
ancients, he could still give due credit to some of the moderns
whenever their contributions seemed valuable.

Temple concludes his essay by speculating on the factors which
have impeded the progress of learning since the Renaissance. The
first is the religious quarrels and wars which have wasted

the Thoughts, the Studies, the Applications, the Endeavours of all or
most of the finest Wits, the deepest Scholars, and the most learned
Writers that the Age produced. Many Excellent Spirits, and the most
Penetrating *Genii*, that might have made admirable Progresses and
Advances in many other Sciences, were sunk and overwhelmed in the

Abyss of Disputes about Matters of Religion, without ever turning their Looks or Thoughts any other Way. To these Disputes of the Pen, succeeded those of the Sword; and the Ambition of great Princes and Ministers, mingled with the Zeal, or covered with the Pretences of Religion, has for a Hundred Years past infested *Christendom* with almost a perpetual Course, or Succession, either of Civil or of Foreign Wars: The Noise and Disorders whereof have been ever the most Capital Enemies of the Muses, who are seated, by the Ancient Fables, upon the Top of *Parnassus;* that is, in a Place of Safety and of Quiet, from the Reach of all Noises and Disturbances of the Regions below. (167)

A second reason has been the indifference of kings and princes toward learning and their consequent failure to patronize it; "I have not observed," Temple says, "in our Modern Story, any Great Princes much celebrated for their Favour of Learning, further than to serve their Turns, to justifie their Pretensions and Quarrels, or flatter their Successes" (168). A third is the rapid growth of European greed since the discovery of America; because avarice cannot raise men's thoughts above the earthy and material, it is "no wonder then, that Learning has been so little advanced since it grew to be Mercenary, and the Progress of it has been fettered by the Cares of the World, and disturbed by the Desires of being rich, or the Fears of being poor" (168).

The greatest obstacle, however, is the "Scorn of Pedantry" which pretentious scholars have brought upon themselves "by pretending to more than they had, or to more Esteem than what they had could [*sic*] deserve, by broaching it in all Places at all Times, upon all Occasions, and by living so much among themselves, or in their Closets and Cells, as to make them unfit for all other Business, and ridiculous in all other Conversations" (168–69). Ridicule directed toward scholarship has also had an ill effect upon learning; similarly, the modern penchant for ridiculing "all that is Serious and Good" has become "the Itch of our Age and Climate, and has overrun both the Court and the State" (169).

Before ending his essay Temple apologizes for his severe manner: "But this is enough to excuse the Imperfections of Learning in our Age, and to censure the Sufficiency of some of the Learned; and this small Piece of Justice I have done the Ancients, will not, I hope, be taken, any more than 'tis meant, for any Injury to the Moderns" (169). Such disarming honesty, however, failed to divert the approaching storm, and soon he was to pay dearly for his comments on the moderns.

The chronology of the consequent controversy needs to be touched upon only lightly here. Temple's essay appeared in 1690, and in 1694 William Wotton, a cleric and an able scholar, published his *Reflections upon Ancient and Modern Learning*, a long work of twenty-nine chapters purporting to investigate the question dispassionately. In general, Wotton thought that in architecture, science, sculpture, painting, logic, philology, and divinity, the moderns are superior, whereas the ancients excelled in politics, ethics, poetry, and oratory. Although some of Temple's friends viewed the book as malice masked by scholarship, Wotton's examination of the evidence was intelligent and fair. In terms of literary scholarship, the book was an important one; for as Miss Burlingame says,

It stands saliently as the first attempt to make a comprehensive investigation by scientific method. Moreover, in extending his enquiry to the Church Fathers, and in attempting to gauge the accuracy of the knowledge which the Ancients had of themselves, Wotton enlarges the field of critical research. As his method is modern, so is his spirit. Dispassionate and fair-minded, he realizes the value of varied contributions to culture, and credits each. While appreciating cultivated scholarship, he never confuses mastery of meticulous details with genius.[5]

After Wottons' book the controversy degenerated into a quarrel over the authenticity of Phalaris' letters and a war of personalities. In 1693–94, young Charles Boyle began work on a scholarly edition of the letters which was published early in 1694 with a preface in which he commented sarcastically upon a real or imagined discourtesy by Richard Bentley, the keeper of the Royal Library at Saint James. A second edition of Wotton's *Reflections* appeared in June, 1697; appended to it was a dissertation by Bentley proving that the epistles of Phalaris were spurious. Boyle and his Christ Church friends answered with a witty and stinging reply entitled *Dr. Bentley's Dissertations on the Epistles of Phalaris and Fables of Aesop Examined by the Hon. C. B.* (1698). But in early 1699 Bentley returned to the battle and effectively put his enemies in their place with his second dissertation. After this the quarrel simmered and cooled, although the two most lasting works to evolve from the controversy, Swift's *The Battle of the Books* and *A Tale of a Tub*, were not published until 1704.

II Some Thoughts upon Reviewing the Essay of Ancient and Modern Learning

During the ensuing quarrel after Wotton's examination Temple, however, did not remain completely aloof. In 1695–96 he started work on an answer to Wotton's discussion, but never finished it. Swift printed it in 1701 in Part III of the *Miscellanea*. Because of the essay's incomplete state, Temple's purpose is not clear, but *Some Thoughts upon Reviewing the Essay of Ancient and Modern Learning*, though not noteworthy for any new ideas, does show his persistence in attempting to discredit the claims of the moderns. He begins by stating his ostensible purpose for writing the essay:

First, the common Interest of Learning in general, and particularly in our Universities; and to prevent the Discouragement of Scholars, in all Degrees, from reading the Antient Authors who must be acknowledged to have been the Foundation of all Modern Learning, whatever the Superstructures may have been. Next, a just Indignation at the Insolence of the Modern Advocates, in defaming those Heroes among the Antients, whose Memory has been sacred and admired for so many Ages; as *Homer, Virgil, Pythagoras, Democritus,* &c. . . . My last Motive was, to vindicate the credit of our Nation, as others have done that of the *French*, from the Imputation of this Injustice and Presumption that the Modern Advocates have used in this case. (*Works,* I, 290)

He then reviews the history of the controversy and defends his ancient heroes—Pythagoras, the Seven Sages, Empedocles, and Democritus—against their modern attackers (290–94). His defense is lifeless and stilted; the modern reader is likely to feel himself treading familiar ground of the earlier essay. Even so, we must admire the old man, gallantly constructing a last defense in a losing war.

Temple apparently planned "to examine the Account they [Wotton and other moderns] gave of those Sciences, wherein they affirm the Moderns to excel the Ancients," but there is a hiatus for which Swift supplies a note: "*Here, it is supposed, the Knowledge of the Ancients and Moderns in the Sciences last mentioned was*

*to have been compared; but whether the Author designed to have
gone through such a Work himself, or intended these Papers only
for Hints for some Body else that desired them, is not known"*
(295). Perhaps Temple later tired of the battle and did not wish
to continue it.

The next section of the essay is concerned with the decay of
learning among the ancient nations: the Egyptians and the Assyrians. In passing he comments upon the modern assertion that the
greatness of Greek poetry is due only to eloquence of language:

> They might as well say, the Excellence of Picture comes from the
> Beauty of the Colours; and of Statuary, from the Fineness of the
> Marble; whereas a common Hand, with the finest Colours in the
> world, can paint nothing better than a Sign-Post: and the drawing of
> a Hand in black and white, may be of ten times more Art and Value,
> as well as Beauty, than a common Picture, though never so finely
> Coloured. 'Tis the same thing in Poetry; the Language is but the
> Colouring; 'tis the Conception, the Invention, the Judgment, that give
> the Life and Spirit, as well as Beauty and Force, to a Poem. (298)

He then proposes that the Greek poets after the Ptolemaic dy-
nasty were perhaps inferior to those which came before but adds
cautiously, "we have but too many of them left us to make the
Comparison" (298).

Proceeding on his way, Temple questions whether chemistry,
philology, and divinity can be classified as sciences; and his answer is negative (298–99). From his discussion of philology, he
digresses to a rather caustic dismissal of critics: "I must confess,
that the Criticks are a Race of Scholars I am very little acquainted
with; having always esteemed them but like Brokers, who having
no Stock of their own, set up and trade with that of other Men;
buying here, and selling there, and commonly abusing both Sides,
to make out a little paultry Gain, either of Money or of Credit for
themselves, and care not at whose Cost" (299). But Temple is
careful, however, to commend the Renaissance critics to whom

> we owe the Editions of all the antient Authors, the best Translations
> of many out of Greek, the restoring of the old Copies, maimed with
> Time or Negligence, the correcting of others mistaken in the transcrib-
> ing, the explaining Places obscure, in an Age so ignorant of the Stile

or Customs of the Antients: And in short, endeavouring to recover those old Jewels out of the Dust and Rubbish, wherein they had been so long lost or soiled; to restore them to their native Lustre, and make them appear in their true Light. (299)

Later critics, however, "have turned their Vein, to debase the Credit and Value of the Antients, and raise their own above those, to whom they owe all the little they know." They concern themselves instead with "vain Niceties and captious Cavils" in semantics, chronology, and place of personal names, "all this, to find some Occasion of censuring and defaming such Writers as are, or have been, most esteemed in the World: Raking into slight Wounds where they find any, or scratching till they make some, where there were none before" (299). Temple's later readers could hardly have missed this thinly veiled reference to William Wotton and Richard Bentley.

After a few paragraphs on theology, Temple moves to a comparison of the productions of the ancients and moderns, "the *Persons* and the *Things*." Of the ancients, he praises Epaminondas, Agesilaus, Alcibiades, Philip of Macedon, the two Scipios, Julius Caesar, Trajan, and Marcus Antoninus for "their Fortitude, their Justice, their Prudence, their Temperance, their Magnanimity, their Clemency, their Love to their Country, and the Sacrifice they made of their Lives" (301-2).

Among the "things," Temple awards the laurels to the ancients in poetry, painting, sculpture, eloquence, architecture, and spectacle; the ancients were superior, he says, in "all arts necessary to life and sustenance," medicine, and government (302). The superiority of the ancients is due to the "Force and Influence of Climates, where they have grown" as well as "the long Peace and flourishing Condition of those antient Empires . . . and also to the Freedom of Thought and Enquiry, in the *Grecian* and *Italian* Republics" (303).

The best works of the moderns, however, have been the invention of the lodestone and gunpowder, neither of which has been of much benefit to mankind (303). The other "airy Speculations of those, who have passed for the great Advancers of Knowledge and Learning these last fifty Years," have similarly been of little use to the welfare of mankind:

The Universal Medicine, which will certainly cure all that have it:
The Philosopher's Stone, which will be found out by Men that care
not for Riches: The Transfusion of young Blood into old Men's Veins,
which will make them as gamesom as the Lambs, from which 'tis to
be derived: An Universal Language, which may serve all Mens Turn,
when they have forgot their own: The Knowledge of one anothers
Thoughts without the grievous Trouble of Speaking: The Art of Fly-
ing, till a Man happens to fall down and break his Neck: Double-bot-
tom'd Ships, whereof none can ever be cast away, besides the first
that was made: The admirable Virtues of that noble and necessary
juice called Spittle, which will come to be sold, and very cheap, in
the Apothecaries Shops: Discoveries of new Worlds in the Planets,
and Voyages between this and that in the Moon, to be made as frequently as between *York* and *London:* Which such poor Mortals as I
am think as wild as those of *Ariosto*, but without half so much Wit, or
so much Instruction; for there, these modern Sages may know, where
they may hope in time to find their lost Senses, preserved in Vials,
with those of *Orlando*. (303)

Shortsighted and opinionated as Temple was, his condemnation
of modern learning was based upon a sincere love of the ancients
and perhaps upon mistaken estimate of the arrogance of the
moderns.

III   *The Dust of an Old Battle*

The quarrel over the merits of the ancients and the moderns
seemed foolish to some of Temple's contemporaries; "T. R., Esq."
(perhaps Thomas Rymer) certainly expressed the feelings of
many when he wrote in his *Essay upon Critical and Curious
Learning* (1698), "If I might advise both parties, they should employ their time and pains upon some more useful subject. There
has been too much dust raised about this already." [6] Even Swift
does not tell us the outcome of the war in *The Battle of the Books,*
other than that Wotton and Bentley are slain by the valiant young
Boyle.

The importance of Temple's participation in the battle of the
books was threefold. First, his attack on modern learning reflected
a strong reaction to the claims of many modern writers, whose
smugness and self-love he found nauseous. Secondly, he could not
accept the modernist doctrine of progress. All of his reading, his
experience, and his observations on men and manners made the

idea both untenable and unpalatable. Finally, he unintentionally stimulated the writing of two of the greatest satires in English literature, Swift's *Battle of the Books* and *A Tale of a Tub*.

Unfortunately, the major result of the controversy was that Temple's reputation as an able diplomat and a fluent writer was eclipsed by that of the clumsy scholar; and, as a result, the worthwhile elements in his other essays have been too often forgotten by later generations. But perhaps he was not as wrong as some might think: he was protesting against those who would confuse material progress with moral or spiritual amelioration and who would puff themselves with pride for that reason.

Temple's last three efforts at writing were largely unhappy and unsuccessful. *The Introduction to the History of England* rapidly slid into obscurity, and the two essays on learning only embroiled him in unpleasant and unwelcome controversy. Somewhat mixed indeed must have been his feelings about literature and critics when he died on January 27, 1699.

CHAPTER 8

Temple and Swift

ONE aspect of Temple's life is briefly touched upon in almost every history of English literature—his patronage of Jonathan Swift. Although the mountain of scholarship dealing with almost every aspect of the life and work of Swift has grown prodigiously during the last thirty years, and although it is possible that we know—or think we know—more about Swift than he did himself about his politics, religion, social attitudes, and economics, there is, nevertheless, very little known about his relationship with Temple, partially because it has been ignored and partially because the necessary materials for a complete study are nonexistent.

Swift spent the better part of the decade from 1689 to 1699 in Temple's service at Moor Park, both as a secretary and as a friend. But aside from a few articles, notes, and passing comments in longer works, scholarship has deftly sidestepped any attempt to assess the possible extent of Temple's influence on Swift's mind and art; but we need in this study to indicate those areas in which Swift might have felt the influence of Temple: politics, natural and moral philosophy, and the conflict between ancient and modern learning. First, however, it is necessary to chart briefly the course of Swift's association with Temple.

I Swift at Moor Park

Just when young Swift, fleeing the disturbances in Ireland occasioned by the Revolution in 1688, arrived at Sheen, we do not know. Certainly he was with Temple by June, 1689; for in that month he wrote a Pindaric ode in which he praised his master for his diplomacy, his keen insight into politics, and his peaceful retirement.[1] Swift's family relationship to Temple probably played some part in his employment because, according to two of his early biographers, his mother was a distant relative of Lady Temple.[2]

Swift's first employment with Temple lasted a little less than a year, and we have little information about his duties during this period except for comments in two letters. Temple, writing to his friend Sir Robert Southwell in 1690, says that the young man "has lived in my house, read to mee, writ for mee, and kept all accounts as farr as my small occasions required." [3] Swift, writing to Lady Giffard in 1709 to refute her charges that he did not use original manuscripts in editing Temple's works, states that the second parts of the *Miscellanea* (1690) and the *Memoirs* (1691), as well as later works, were "from my Copy. . . . They were all copied from the Originals by Sr Wm Temples direction, and corrected all along by his Orders." [4] Thus as early as 1690 Swift was already making his acquaintance with the works which were to exert some influence on his own thinking.

Not content with copying out another's work, Swift was making his first efforts at writing poetry in his spare hours. His "Ode to Sir William Temple" is dated from Moor Park in June, 1689; but it was not published until 1745, the year of Swift's death. The poem itself is not striking except for the insight it gives us into Swift's early attitude toward Temple. As we might expect, it is so full of praise and admiration that the modern reader is apt to smile while reading that Temple possesses those qualities "Learn'd, Good, and Great,/Which we ne'er join'd before, but in Romances meet" (ll. 59–60). [5] Swift mourns that the court is ruled by deceit and that virtue has fled the kingdom; nevertheless, Temple has saved England by keeping her at peace: "You bought it at a cheaper Rate;/Nor has it left the usual bloody Scar,/To shew it cost its Price in War" (ll. 73–75). Temple has retired to his garden at Moor Park, "tir'd with loss of Time and Ease" (l. 133), having striven unsuccessfully to "cultivate a barren Court in vain" (l. 175). Obsequious as the poem may seem to some, Swift's admiration for Temple is certainly evident, even at this early stage of their relationship.

Swift left Moor Park sometime before May, 1690, to return to Ireland for reasons of health. As he tells us in the "Fragment of an Autobiography," "For he [Swift] happened, before twenty years old, by a surfeit of fruit, to contract a giddiness and coldness of stomach, that almost brought him to his grave. . . . Upon this occasion he returned to Ireland, in 1690, by advice of Physicians, who weakly imagined that his native air might be of some use to recover his health." [6] Realizing Swift's usefulness as an intelligent editorial assistant, Temple was understandably hesitant to part with him; but he nevertheless wrote the letter to Southwell, who was going to Ireland as secretary of state. Dated at Moor Park on May 29, 1690, the letter says in part, "He has latine and greeke some French, writes a very good and current hand, is very honest and diligent, and has good friends though they have for the present lost their fortunes in Ireland and his whole family having been long known to mee thus farr to take care of Him." [7] The two men undoubtedly parted on good terms, for Swift was soon to return.

The autumn of 1691 found Swift back in England, visiting his mother in Leicestershire and his cousin Thomas at Oxford. Sometime before the beginning of 1692, he was again with Temple, but the reasons for his return to Moor Park are unclear. Soon afterward we find him writing to Thomas Swift of his admiration for Temple: "I never read his writings but I prefer him to all others at present in England, Which I suppose is all but a piece of selflove, and the likeness of humours makes one fond of them as if they were ones own." [8] Swift probably resumed his former duties, including those of reading copy for Temple, who, if Swift's letter to Lady Giffard is correct, was preparing his *Introduction to the History of England.*[9]

The three important events of Swift's second tenure with Temple were his taking of the master of arts degree from Oxford, his appearance before King William to present Temple's written arguments in favor of the Triennial Bill (which provided for Parliamentary elections every three years), and his decision to seek his vocation in the church. The later two are of major importance in Swift's development, for his meeting with the king was probably his first exposure to practical politics, and his entry into the Church of England determined to a large extent the course of his subsequent career as a political pamphleteer.

Entering Oxford University as a member of Hart Hall on June 14, 1692, and taking no examinations by reason of having qualified at Trinity College in 1689, he received his degree on July 5. Apparently he enjoyed the experience, for he wrote to William Swift on November 29, concerning his treatment at Oxford, "I had all the civilities I could wish for, and so many [showed me] favours, that I am ashamed to have been more obliged in a few weeks to strangers, than ever I was in seven years to Dublin College." [10] Temple apparently assisted him in receiving the degree[11] and promised to use his influence with the king to get him a prebend, a promise that later caused some bitterness on Swift's part.[12]

The political debate over the Triennial Bill in 1693 was the occasion for Swift's first political experience. King William, who was undecided as to whether he should pass the bill, finally sent the Earl of Portland to Temple for advice. Temple persisted in favoring the bill; and, as Swift tells us,

Whereupon Mr. Swift was sent to Kenington with the whole account of the matter in writing to convince the King and the Earl of Portland how ill they were informed. He told the Earl, to whom he was referred by his Majesty (and gave it in writing) that the ruin of King Charles I was now owing to his passing the Triennial Bill, which did not hinder him from dissolving any parliament, but to the passing of another bill, which put it out of his power to dissolve the parliament then in being, without consent of the house. Mr. Swift, who was well-versed in English history, although he was under twenty-one years old, gave the King a short account of the matter, but a more large one to the Earl of Portland; but all in vain. For the King by ill advisers was prevailed upon to refuse passing the bill.[13]

The failure of this mission evidently loomed large in Swift's memory, for he ends his account by remarking that this "was the first time that Mr. Swift had ever any converse with courts, and he told his friends that it was the first incident that helped to cure him of vanity." [14]

Swift made his second departure from Moor Park in May, 1694, as a result of his decision to enter the church. The decision was not a sudden one, for as early as February, 1692, in a letter to John Kendall, a clergyman, he had indicated that he was thinking of taking orders.[15] By November 29 of the same year his inclination has become a resolution; he writes to William Swift, "I am not to take orders till the King gives me a Prebendary: and Sir William Temple, tho' he promises me the certainty of it, yet is less forward than I could wish; because, I suppose he believes I shall leave him, and upon some accounts, he thinks me a little necessary to him [at present]." [16]

The exact terms of the promised preferment are not known, but Swift seems to have been convinced that the promise had been made. Louis A. Landa says that Swift may have expected a prebend in either Canterbury or Westminster, and that his impatience is therefore understandable; for these royal prebends, with their attractive revenues and their slight residence obligations, were much sought after; and either one would have made Swift financially secure.[17] The period of delay between 1692 and his ordination in 1694 can probably be interpreted as a time during which he waited anxiously for preferment in England, one which did not come at this time and which would never come.

Swift's suspicions proved correct: Temple was so eager to retain him that he consequently offered him a more independent position in his office as master of the rolls in Ireland. Swift, however, declined and left Moor Park sometime in May, 1694, after a heated parting, as we learn from a letter to Deane Swift (the father of Swift's early biographer): "I forgot to tell You I left Sir William Temple a month ago, just as I foretold it to You, and every thing happened thereupon exactly as I guest. He was extream angry I left Him, and yet would not oblige himself any further than upon my good Behaviour, nor would promise any thing firmly to Me at all; so that every Body judged I did best to leave Him." [18] Biographers have tended to see in this letter evidence of a strained relationship of long standing between the two men, but a more reasonable view is that Temple's reaction was merely that of a man suddenly faced with the loss of a trusted and competent employee.

Swift, however, was still not finished with Temple; on October 6, 1694, he found it necessary to write to his patron from Dublin, asking him to send a "certificate of behaviour" to the Archbishop of Dublin so that his ordination could proceed. In this so-called penitential letter, which some biographers have twisted into rather flimsy evidence of enmity between the two men, Swift requests that

Your Honor will . . . please to send to me some Certificate of my Behaviour during almost three Years in Your Family: Wherein I shall stand in need of all Your Goodness to excuse my Many Weaknesses and Follyes and Oversights; much more, to say any Thing to my Advantage. The Particulars expected of me, are what relate, to Morals and Learning, and the Reasons of quitting your Honor's Family, that is, whether the last was occasion'd by any ill Actions of mine. They are all entirely left to Your Honor's Mercy, thô in the first, I think I cannot reproach my self any further than for Infirmityes.[19]

Temple's letter is not extant, but he undoubtedly wrote one, for on October 28 Swift was ordained a deacon. On January 23, 1695, he became a priest, and two weeks later he was appointed to the prebend of Kilroot in the cathedral of Connor.

Swift's second tenure at Moor Park was busy and profitable. His interest in poetry hardly slackened, for in this period he wrote five poems which have come down to us and probably composed three others. His first published poem, "Ode to the Athenian Society," appeared in the fifth volume of John Dunton's *Athenian Gazette* (1692). A second ode, this one celebrating King William's victory over the Irish at the Boyne in 1690, was printed in the *Gentleman's Journal* in July 1692. Three other early pieces, "To Mr. Congreve," "Ode to Dr. William Sancroft," and the poem "Occasioned by Sir W—— T——'s Late Illness and Recovery," were not published until 1789. Generally, these poems are labored and artificial, though not without occasional glimmers of promise. In light of Swift's later artistry as a satirical poet and his fluency with the couplet, these odes seem sluggishly imitative and dull.

However, the poem on Temple's illness, written in December, 1693, is valuable as an indicator of Swift's attitude toward the older man. Temple was often the victim of gout, and this time he was apparently in a serious condition, for Swift writes that

> As parent earth, burst by imprison'd winds,
> Scatters strange agues o'er men's sickly minds,
> And shakes the atheist's knees; such ghastly fear
> Late I beheld on every face appear. (ll. 37–40)[20]

Lady Temple ("Mild Dorothea") "Trembling beheld the doubtful hand of fate," while Grief traces her "watery footsteps" in the face of Lady Giffard ("Dorinda"). But even while the household rejoices over the master's recovery, Swift is still melancholy. Actually, his own sadness has little to do with Temple; instead, he is distressed by his lack of success as a poet and speaks of the Muse as a malignant goddess, the "universal cause of all my woe" (l. 82). This unhappiness over his poetry doubtless explains in part his decision to leave Temple a second time.

Three other poems of this period are not extant. Writing to Thomas Swift on May 3, 1692, he says, "This Virgil sticks plaguily on my hands, I did about 200 lines and gave it to my Lady G. for

a Sample, and she and Sr W. T. like it as I would have them. . . .
I will send you something I writt to a young lady in Ireland
which I call the Ramble." [21] And in the ode "To Mr. Congreve"
(ll. 205–12) he quotes some lines from an earlier poem entitled
"The Poet." [22]

Swift's restlessness was not relieved when he left Moor Park, for
his life at Kilroot was weary and unrewarding; the stipend was
more than one handred pounds a year, but the decline into which
the diocese of Connor had fallen during the seventeenth century
was another factor which probably hastened his decision to return
to Temple.[23] Temple probably extended an invitation for his return in April, 1696, and a month later Swift left Kilroot for England. According to Jane Swift, his sister, he went to Moor Park
with the expectation of another appointment in the church
through Temple's influence, but again preferment did not come.

During his last stay with Temple, Swift continued his former
routine, but he was also using his leisure hours to read in Temple's
magnificent library, as a list of books he read in 1697 and early
1698 shows.[24] The titles listed are of great interest, for they indicate his intellectual bent at this time. A great many of the classics
are on the list: Aelian, Cicero, Diodorus Siculus, Homer, Horace,
Lucius Florus, Lucretius, Petronius Arbiter, Theophrastus, Thu-
cydides, and Vergil. There are also the Church Fathers Cyprian
and Irenaeus. Almost as numerous as the classics are the books by
modern historians: Burnet's *History of the Reformation*, William
Camden's *Annals of Elizabeth*, Lord Herbert of Cherbury's *Life
and Raigne of Henry VIII*, Johannes Sleidanus' *Commentariorus
de statu religionis et reipublicae, Carolo V. Caesare*, and Vossius'
De historicis Graecis and *De historicis Latinus*, along with several
anonymous works: *Histoire de M. Constance, Histoire d'Aethi-
ope*, and *Histoire de Chypre*. Other books listed are Sir Richard
Blackmore's *Prince Arthur*, Sir John Davies *Of the Soul* (*Nosce
Teipsum*), a volume of the works of Vincent Voiture, Fontenelle's
Dialogues des Morts, François Bernier's *Grand Mogul*, two volumes of Jeremy Collier's essays, and two anonymous travel books,
the *Voyage de Syam* and the *Voyage de Maroc*. Of great interest
is the fact that no scientific books are included. The presence of
any works on natural philosophy in Temple's library is doubtful
because of his antagonism toward science.

Swift's last residence with Temple was probably the most fruitful in terms of his literary career, for during this period he wrote *The Battle of the Books* and *A Tale of a Tub*, neither of which was published, however, until 1704. Concerning *A Tale of a Tub*, he says in the "Apology," written for the fifth edition (1710), that the "greatest Part of that Book was finished above thirteen Years since, 1696, which is eight Years before it was published," [25] and modern editors have generally agreed with this statement. The dating of *The Battle of the Books* is no less certain; in "The Bookseller to the Reader" he tells us that "The following Discourse . . . seems to have been written about the same time with the former, I mean, the Year 1697, when the famous Dispute was on Foot, about Antient and Modern Learning." [26]

The background of the controversy between the ancients and the moderns has been covered in Chapter 7. It is sufficient, for the present, to point out that Swift's entrance into the conflict was a direct result of his close association with Temple over a period of several years. Silly as Swift may have thought certain aspects of the squabble to be, he could not stand idly by and leave his master defenseless against the pedantic onslaughts of Bentley and Wotton.

Temple's death closed the first portion of Swift's career, and it was an important one. In recording the event, he reveals much of his attitude toward the man to whom he had been so close during the past decade: "He died at one o'clock this morning . . . , and with him all that was good and amiable among men." [27] A little later, he expanded his statement: "He was a person of the greatest wisdom, justice, liberality, politeness, eloquence of his age and nation; the truest lover of his country, and one that deserved far more from it by his eminent public services than may man before or since: besides his great deserving of the commonwealth of learning; having been universally esteemed the most accomplished writer of his time." [28] Thus, at the age of thirty-one Swift found himself without a patron and without any position which would assure his livelihood. However, Temple did provide for him in two ways which reveal the esteem in which he held the younger man. First, in a codicil to his will dated February 2, 1698, Temple left one hundred pounds to Swift.[29] He also granted him the right to publish his collected writings, though this was not stated in the will. Swift remained at Moor Park only a few months after Temple's burial, and by July, 1699, he was chaplain to Lord Berkeley, the newly appointed lord justice for Ireland.

After his departure from Moor Park, Swift continued to have occasional relations with the Temple family, not all of them pleasant. He edited and published the third part of Temple's *Miscellanea* (1701) and the third part of the *Memoirs* (1709); the delay in the publication of the latter was probably occasioned by Swift's desire, or perhaps by a promise to Temple, to wait until all those unfavorably mentioned were dead.[30] For this work, Swift received approximately forty pounds for each of the five volumes.[31]

The publication of these works soon brought him into conflict with Lady Giffard; he had sold the manuscript of the *Memoirs* to Benjamin Tooke, the printer, without consulting her. She had in her possession the original manuscript in Temple's hand but had refused to lend it to Swift. When the volume was printed, she wrote to him and accused him of editing the work from an "unfaithful" copy. He received her letter on October 6, 1709, and replied about a month later. He ably defends himself and his actions:

Your Ladyship says, if ever they were designed to be printed, it must have been from the Originall. Nothing of his ever printed in my Time was from the Originall; the first Memoirs was from my Copy; so were the Second Miscellanea: so was the Introduction to the English History: so was every Volume of Letters, They were all copied from the Originals by Sr Wm Temples direction, and corrected all along by his Orders; and it was the same with these last Memoirs: So that whatever be printed since I had the Honor to know him, was an unfaithfull Copy if it must be tryed by the Originall. Madam; I pretend not to have had the least Share in Sr Wm Temples Confidence above his Relations or his commonest Friends; (I have but too good Reason to think otherwise). . . . Nobody else had conversed so much with his Manuscripts as I, and since I was not wholly illiterate, I cannot imagine whom else he could leave the Care of his Writings to.[32]

Although Swift was probably not as circumspect as he should have been, the charges of vanity and dishonesty which Julia Longe, Lady Giffard's biographer, presses against him are in the main untrue.[33] Understandably, Swift and Lady Giffard remained cool toward each other.

His relations with the rest of the Temple family were apparently cordial but not intimate. John Temple, Sir William's nephew, corresponded with him several times and in 1706 invited him to Moor Park. Swift declined the invitation but added gracefully, "I am extremely obliged by yr kind Invitation to More-Park, wch no time will make me forgot [sic] or love less." [34] If the two men corresponded again before 1737, the letters are not extant. In this year Swift wrote to Temple from Dublin, requesting financial aid for Rebecca Dingley and mentioning his gift of Lady Giffard's portrait to Temple. Part of the letter is quite nostalgic:

> I am sorry to have been so much a stranger to the state of your family. I know nothing of your lady or what children you have, or any other circumstances. . . . I very much approve of your keeping up your family-house at *Moor-park*. I have heard it is very much changed for the better, as well as the gardens. The tree on which I carved those words, *factura nepotibus umbram*, is one of those elms that stand in the hollow ground just before the house; but I suppose the letters are widened and grown shapeless by time.[35]

There is no evidence that Swift had dealings with any other branch of the Temple family.

References to Temple are exceedingly rare in Swift's later correspondence; when they do occur, they are always brief and usually somewhat obscure in their reference, falling into no coherent pattern. In the *Journal to Stella* he twice mentions Temple's refusal to become secretary of state: "I am thinking what a veneration we used to have for Sir William Temple, because he might have been secretary of state at fifty," and, later, "I have often thought about what a splutter Sir William Temple makes about being secretary of State." [36] Another reference shows that his relationship with Temple was not without those momentary frictions which afflict even the closest friendships: "I would not be treated like a school-boy; . . . I had felt too much of that in my life already (meaning from Sir William Temple)," and just a short while later, "Don't you remember how I used to be in pain when Sir William Temple would look cold and out of humour for three or four days, and I used to suspect a hundred reasons? I have pluckt up my spirit since then, faith; he spoiled a fine gentleman." [37] But his final reference in the Journal recalls lighter moments at Moor Park: "Ld Treasr has hd an ugly fit of the Rheumatism, but is now near quite well, I was playing at one and thirty with him and his Family tother night. he gave us all 12 pence apiece to begin with: it put me in mind of Sr W. T." [38] Swift's temperament, however, would have made it hard for him to find happiness anywhere; and Stephen Gwynn is right in believing that Moor Park and Temple had "brought into his cloudy life the best sunshine that it was to know." [39]

II Temple's Influence on Swift

Swift's personal happiness at Moor Park would be of minor consequence for us if it did not parallel his intellectual growth under Temple's patronage. W. D. Taylor states the case very convincingly: "In these ten years his genius was gathering nourishment and strength. . . . Swift got food for his intellect at Moor Park. There was laid the train on which his mind was to explode . . ." [40] The years at Moor Park were ones in which Swift was influenced both positively and negatively by Temple in varying degrees, in certain aspects of his thinking on politics, on moral and natural philosophy, and on the controversy between the ancients and the moderns.

Some of Swift's ideas on the origin and nature of government, especially in such early work as Contests and Dissensions in Ancient Rome and Athens (1701), were strongly influenced by Temple. Both men found the origins of government in the evolution of the patriarchal system; and both rejected, either directly or implicitly, the social contract theories of Hooker, Hobbes, Harrington, and Locke. Like Temple, Swift was willing to grant the ruler a great reservoir of authority which has its source in the consent and continued goodwill of the people. Although both men seemed inclined toward monarchy as the most workable form of government, they were in reality proponents of the mixed state theory which had as its central thesis the necessity of a balance of power among the various components of the state. Finally, both stood in fear of the ever-present specters of political factions and standing armies. [41]

Certainly, most of these political ideas were part of the intellectual heritage of the seventeenth century; but the close personal relationship of the two men and the frequent verbal parallels in their works rule out the suggestion of mere coincidence. If Robert J. Allen and Irvin Ehrenpreis are correct in suggesting that Swift drew upon Temple's person and works—especially upon the essays on government and popular discontents—for the writing of his first political essay (*Contests and Dissensions . . . in Athens and Rome*, 1701) and for his sketch of the King of Brobdingnag in Book II of *Gulliver's Travels*,[42] the probability of Temple's influence becomes even stronger.

The impress of Temple's ideas seems equally clear in Swift's attitude toward science, particularly in certain passages of *The Battle of the Books, A Tale of a Tub,* and *Gulliver's Travels.* Specifically, Temple's thinking is reflected in Swift's questioning of the significance of the experiments of the scientists, in his satiric adaptations of projects ascribed to the virtuosi by Temple, in his distrust of physicians and their prescriptions, in his borrowing from certain volumes of the *Philosophical Transactions,* and in his use of certain details from Temple's life and thought for his portrait of Lord Munodi in Book III of *Gulliver's Travels.* Like Temple, he looked upon natural philosophy as a fad short-lived and ill-fitted to the relief of human misery.[43]

Furthermore, there can be little doubt that Swift was influenced by Temple in writing *The Battle of the Books* and *A Tale of a Tub.* Consciously or not, he was influenced by Temple's prejudices as he selected the combatants of the two armies in *The Battle of the Books.*[44] In *A Tale of a Tub* he reflects Temple's attitudes toward the modern critics and their work, particularly in his praise of those who restore or improve and in his condemnation of those who only find fault in order to bolster their own lagging fortunes and reputations.[45]

But there is one area in Swift's thought to which Temple probably contributed in a negative way. This is his violent attack upon the Epicurean concept of the pleasurable life in *A Tale of a Tub,* the idea with which he was no doubt familiar through his reading while revising and editing Temple's *Upon the Gardens of Epicurus.* Ignoring such vital Epicurean doctrines as the rejection of immortality and Providence, the insistence upon the material basis of truth, and the atomic structure of matter, Swift, like Temple, concentrated solely upon the ethic of Epicurus—Swift to attack it, and Temple to praise. This focus upon Epicurean ethics

suggests that Swift's lifelong antagonism toward Epicurean morality was first stimulated by his reading of Temple's essay on gardening.[46]

These factors suggest that Temple was a strong influence on
Swift's mind and art, though by no means the only one or even the
strongest one. Certainly there were other factors, other persons,
and other ideas in Swift's later years which were to modify or to
extend his insights into the problems of mankind; but at Moor
Park under the beneficence of Temple the world of the intellect
first opened to Swift.

CHAPTER 9

Afterfame

D URING the two and a half centuries since his death, Temple has slipped from literary prominence in his own time to comparative obscurity in the late nineteenth and twentieth centuries. A quick glance at his bibliography indicates that in 1699 and throughout the eighteenth century his works enjoyed a large audience.[1] As we have seen, Swift's comments, written shortly after his friend's death, are indicative of the impressions Temple's person and writings could leave in a sensitive and critical mind,[2] but his praise is the highest given to Temple before the twentieth century. As decades passed, his place in literary importance gradually declined.

The seeds of Temple's decline were probably sown while he was still alive. In 1694, Wotton published his *Reflections upon Ancient and Modern Learning*, which, despite the author's claim to impartiality, was an attack on Temple's championing of the ancients. Although Wotton could agree with Temple that the ancients probably surpassed their successors in literature and most of the arts, he asserts that the moderns have excelled the ancients in science and mathematics. More than one-third of his book is devoted to a refutation of Temple's arguments, and he examines Temple's evidence with a great degree of fairness. Nevertheless, Temple's scholarship was now suspect for the first time; and Richard Bentley's first *Dissertation upon the Epistles of Phalaris*, appended to a second edition of Wotton's *Reflections* in 1697, sharpened the suspicions. Temple's attempted reply to Wotton was never completed; Swift published it in the third part of the *Miscellanea* as *Some Thoughts upon Reviewing the Essay of Ancient and Modern Learning*.

Temple's reputation remained high during the eighteenth century. Shortly after his death, his works continued to appear, some of them for the first time. From 1700 to 1709 Swift published five volumes of letters, memoirs, and essays. In 1700 he edited *Letters Written by Sir W. Temple, Bart, and Other Ministers of State* in two volumes. The letters, which cover Temple's activities from 1665 to 1672, are accompanied by a "Publisher's Epistle" in which Swift comments perceptively on Temple's style:

It is generally believed, that this Author, has advanced our English Tongue, to as great a perfection as it can well bear; and yet, how great a Master he was of it, has I think, never appeared so much, as it will in the following Letters; wherein the Style appears so very different, according to the difference of the Persons, to whom they were address'd; either Men of Business, or Idle; of Pleasure, or Serious; of great or of less Parts or Abilities, in their several Stations. So, that, one may discover, the Characters of most of those Persons, he writes to, from the Stile of his Letters.[3]

In the next year Swift published the third part of the *Miscellanea*, undoubtedly to capitalize on Temple's continuing popularity, but the preface to the volume says little about Temple. Another volume of letters, *Letters to the King, the Prince of Orange, the Chief Ministers of State, and Other Persons*, appeared in 1703, again without noteworthy comment. But in his preface to the *Memoirs*, Part III (1709), Swift praises the historical merit of the book against possible detractors and defends Temple's gallicisms:

it is to be consider'd, that at the Treaty of *Nimeguen,* all Business, either by Writing or Discourse, pass'd in the *French* Tongue; and the Author having liv'd so many Years abroad in that and former Ambassys, where all Business, as well as Conversation ran in that Language, it was hardly possible for him to write upon Publick Affairs without some Tincture of it in his Style; tho' in his other Writings, there be little or nothing of it to be observ'd: And as he often assur'd me it was a Thing he never affected; so upon the Objections made to his former Memoirs, he blotted out some *French* Words in these, and plac'd *English* in their stead, tho' perhaps not so significant.[4]

Thus Swift, who had been so close to Temple for a decade, continued to look with pride upon the work of his late patron.

Swift was not the only person in the early part of the century to admire Temple's writing. John Hughes, in *Of Style* (1698), lists

Temple with Bishop Thomas Sprat and Archbishop John Tillotson as the three "most correct Writers" of prose[5] and says that Temple's style "is very harmonious and sweet, full of Spirit, and *Raciness of Wit*, to use a Word of his own. His Similies are particularly fine, his Allusions graceful, his Words significant, and the whole has a kind of Charm, which amuses the Reader with serious Pleasure, puts him in a good Humour while he is reading, and leaves him thoughtful when he breaks off.[6] In this same essay, Hughes refers to Temple's first essay on ancient and modern learning,[7] and in his *Essay on Allegorical Poetry* (1715) he quotes Temple's strictures against the "rules" to show that they would not be of any help to writers of allegory;[8] nevertheless, he is puzzled by Temple's comments about Spenser.[9]

The tendency to quote Temple was not uncommon elsewhere in the century. Richard Steele in *Guardian* No. 144 (Wednesday, August 26, 1713) employs a quotation from Temple's essay on poetry to strengthen his own theory of English humor;[10] and Samuel Say, in *An Essay on the Harmony, Variety, and Power of Numbers, Whether in Prose or Verse* (1745) cites Temple's etymology of *rime* as a corruption of *rune* rather than the Greek *rhythmus*.[11] Even Oliver Goldsmith could plagiarize Temple's famous concluding lines from the essay on poetry for *The Good Natur'd Man* (1768): "Life is at the greatest and best but a froward child, that must be humour'd and coax'd a little till it falls asleep, and then all the care is over." [12]

Temple was not only quoted; he was also looked back upon as one of the leading writers and critics of his age. Leonard Welsted, in *A Dissertation Concerning the Perfection of the English Language, the State of Poetry, etc.* (1724), speaks of Horace and Temple as "Two authorities of . . . any weight with men of sense" and quotes Temple's first essay on learning: "The least grain of wit one is born with is worth all the improvements one can afterwards make by study." [13]

Two of the eighteenth-century literary giants, Alexander Pope and Samuel Johnson, held Temple in high esteem. Pope's comments are recorded in Joseph Spence's *Anecdotes* (published 1820). In Section VIII (1743–44) he cites Temple as an authority on vocabulary: "In most doubts, whether a word is English or not, or whether such a particular use of it is proper, one has nothing but authority for it. Is it in Sir William Temple, or Locke, or Tillotson?—If it be, you may conclude that it is right, or at least won't be looked upon as wrong." [14] Pope also tells us that in his earlier years he had read and enjoyed Temple's essays, except for those dealing with political subjects: "In my first setting out, I never read any Art of Logic or Rhetoric. I met with Locke, he was quite insipid to me. I read Sir William Temple's Essays too then, but whenever there was anything political in them, I had no manner of feeling for it." [15]

Johnson was even more enthusiastic about Temple. Boswell records: "He once told me, that he had formed his style upon that of Sir William Temple, and upon Chamber's Proposal for his Dictionary. He was certainly mistaken; or if he imagined at first that he was imitating Temple, he was very unsuccessful; for nothing can be more unlike than the simplicity of Temple, and the richness of Johnson. Their styles differ as plain cloth and brocade." [16] Boswell preferred to believe that Johnson's style owed more to Hooker, Bacon, Sanderson, and Hakewell, but Hill and Powell have shown some interesting stylistic parallels in the writings of Temple and Johnson.[17]

Johnson also gave Temple a prominent place in English literary history, telling Boswell, David Garrick, and James Harris on April 9, 1778, that "Sir William Temple was the first writer who gave cadence to English prose. Before his time they were careless of arrangement, and did not mind whether a sentence ended with an important word or an insignificant word, or with what part of speech it was concluded." [18] Thus Johnson shared the opinions of Swift and Hughes about the importance of Temple's style.

Johnson also found Temple a convenient source of wisdom, quotations, and allusions. In his "Preface to the Preceptor," he lists Temple as one of the political writers a young English gentleman must read if he is to "Obtain such knowledge as may qualify him to act and judge as one of a free people." The others Johnson recommends are Sir John Fortescue, Sir Nicholas Bacon, John Locke, and Richard Hooker.[19] Boswell also records Johnson's quotations of, and allusions to, Temple's essays on four occasions.[20]

The praise of Swift, Hughes, Welsted, Say, Steele, and Johnson was not shared by all eighteenth-century writers, however. Gilbert Burnet's *History of His Own Times* (posthumously, 1724–34) attacks Temple's personality, religion, and ethics:

He was a vain man, much puffed up in his own conceit, which he showed indecently on all occasions. He had a true judgment in affairs, and very good principles in relation to government, but good in nothing else, *for he was an Epicurean both in principle and practice;* he seemed to think that things were as they are, from all eternity; at least he thought religion was fit only for the mob. He was a great admirer of the sect of Confucius, in China, who were atheists themselves, but left religion to the rabble. He was a corrupter of all that came near him, and he delivered himself wholly to study, ease, and pleasure.[21]

Courtenay attributes this attack to the Bishop's jealousy of King William's confidence in Temple and to Burnet's characteristic flippancy.[22] Swift, in his marginalia to Burnet's book, remarks acidly, "Sir William Temple was a man of virtue, to which Burnet was a stranger." [23]

Others in the century, particularly Charles Gildon and David Hume, were also unfavorably inclined toward Temple. Gildon, in *The Complete Art of Poetry*, Dialogue II (1718), having discarded the liberal attitude toward the "rules" found in his *Miscellaneous Letters and Essays* (1694), employs Temple's arguments against the rules in the speeches of Tyro, one of the participants in the discussion. Tyro is answered at length by Laudon, who asserts that Temple contradicts himself:

Here you find Sir *William* denying Perfection to *Poetry*, without it be instructed by Art; but if he mean any thing by *Art*, he means what every Body in the World means by it, that ever made use of that Word on any occasion. Now every *Art* in its very Constitution proposes some certain *End* to obtain, and some certain *Means* of Obtaining that *End;* but the Means in Art of *Poetry*, as well as in all others, are what we call the Rules of the *Art*. So that to talk of the Necessity of Art, and at the same Time disallow of its *Rules* is downright Nonsense; or the proposing an *End*, without any *Means* of attaining that *End*, which is equally absurd and ridiculous.[24]

Laudon further asks whether insistence upon care, elegance, exactness, industry, and art in writing does not confine literature "to certain Rules." And to drive home his point he defends the French advocates of the "rules" and scores Temple for believing that there were no great poets in Greece and Rome after Aristotle and Horace published their "rules." [25] In the eyes of Laudon (and Gil-

don), Lord Roscommon, who translated Horace's *Ars Poetica*, is a
"much greater Man, in his Way," than Temple and "other
Enemies to the Rules." [26]

David Hume, who comments on Temple in his essay *Of Liberty
and Despotism* (1741) and in his *History of England* (1754–61),
shows little regard in the essay for Temple's writing: "As to
Sprat, Temple and Locke, they knew too little of the Rules of Art
to be esteem'd elegant Writers." [27] Later, in the history, he is
somewhat more lenient; speaking of Restoration writers, he says:

> Of all the considerable writers of this age, Sir William Temple is
> almost the only one that kept himself altogether unpolluted by that
> inundation of vice and licentiousness which overwhelmed the nation.
> The style of this author, though extremely negligent, and even infected
> with foreign idioms, is agreeable and interesting. That mixture of
> vanity which appears in his works, is rather a recommendation to them.
> By means of it we enter into acquaintance with the character of the
> author, full of honor and humanity; and fancy that we are engaged, not
> in the perusal of a book, but in conversation with a companion.[28]

Hume's ambivalent attitude was indicative of the course Temple's
reputation was to follow in the years to come

Generally, the eighteenth-century estimate of Temple was a favorable one. The opinion of Sir James Mackintosh, writing late in
the century, anticipates a transition to later attitudes: "Swift represents Temple as having brought English style to perfection.
Hume, I think, mentions him; but of late he is not often spoken of
as one of the reformers of our style—this, however, he certainly
was. The structure of his style is perfectly modern." [29] Even
though Mackintosh recognized Temple's significance, his star had
reached its zenith less than a hundred years after his death.

Temple's reputation declined rapidly in the nineteenth century.
Although a major biography and a complete edition of his works
were published in the early part of the century, he was almost
forgotten by 1900. Nevertheless, Temple could still charm some of
his readers. In 1833 Charles Lamb published his *Last Essays of
Elia*, among which "The Genteel Style in Writing" is devoted to
Temple. Lamb begins by comparing the writings of Temple and
Lord Shaftesbury: "Nothing can be more unlike, than the inflated
finical rhapsodies of Shaftesbury and the plain natural chit-chat.

The man of rank is descernible in both writers; but in the one [Temple] it is only insinuated gracefully, in the other [Shaftesbury] it stands out offensively." [30] Throughout the rest of his essay Lamb quotes judiciously and at length from the essays and memoirs to show Temple's grace and ease in writing. Lamb's estimate may be found near the beginning of his essay: "What can be more pleasant than the way in which the retired statesman peeps out in his essays, penned by the latter in his retreat at Shene?" [31]

Three years after the publication of Lamb's essay, Thomas Peregrine Courtenay published the first reliable biography of Temple. The two-volume *Memoirs of the Life, Works, and Correspondence of Sir William Temple, Bart.*, despite occasional errors in fact and interpretation, is still an important source of information for students of Temple's writings. In the years since 1836 scholars, notably Marburg and Woodbridge, have uncovered much additional information in connection with Temple; but Courtenay's biography has lost little of its original value.

Courtenay, like Abel Boyer a hundred years before, was more interested in Temple's diplomacy and politics than in his personality, his family, and his writings. Boyer's *Memoirs of the Life and Negotiations of Sir William Temple* (1714) is little more than a piece of Grub Street writing, held together by long quotations from the memoirs and letters. Courtenay's biography, however, is much more carefully organized and objective than Boyer's. Most of Courtenay's conclusions are found in Chapter XXXVIII. Of Temple's diplomatic work, he says:

We think it no detraction, to say, that even in diplomacy his merit consisted rather in honesty, sincerity, and candour, and in the ability with which he pursued a simple object, than in the grandeur or extent of his schemes of policy. . . . [B]y these he overcame suspicion, and conciliated friendship, and effected easily and quickly, a simple purpose; but in the midst of complicated transactions, managed by skilful and unprincipled diplomatists, and above all directed by a wavering and dishonest government, the fine and amiable qualities of his diplomacy were lost or counteracted. [32]

Courtenay, who is equally admiring of Temple's character, defends him against Burnet's vicious aspersions, [33] and concludes that

Temple's eminence in the lighter qualities of humanity, and the agreeableness of his manner and conversation, would be inferred from the style of his letters, even if his sister had not claimed them for him. We have not presented a faultless hero: but he must, indeed, be a fastidious critic and unreasonable moralist upon whom the blemishes which have been discovered in Sir William Temple have made a deeper impression than his virtues. We might pardon in a statesman or writer, many more of the failings of which Temple is accused, for the honesty, the sincerity, and the patriotism, which characterize his life and works.[34]

Courtenay thus continued the trend of favorable critical and biographical interpretation.

But the tide was soon to turn. Thomas Babington Macaulay, who reviewed Courtenay's biography in October, 1838, used his review as a springboard for the most uncharitable assessments ever made of Temple's person and works. Macaulay, who admits that Courtenay has been diligent, careful, sensible, and impartial, is irritated by his "snarls against the Whigs of the present day." Therefore he states, "We doubt whether it will be found that the memory of Sir William Temple owes much to Mr. Courtenay's researches." [35]

In Macaulay's comments on Temple, which can only be summarized here, he classifies Temple as "one of those men whom the world has agreed to praise highly without knowing much about them, and who are therefore more likely to lose than gain by a close examination." [36] Despite the fact that in profligate and corrupt times "he contracted no great stain and bore no part in any great crime" and that he won esteem without subserviency, Macaulay finds Temple not to his liking: "a temper not naturally good, but under strict command; a constant regard to decorum; a rare caution in playing that mixed game of skill and hazard, human life; a disposition to be content with small and certain winnings rather than to go on doubling the stake." [37] And later:

Temple, we fear, had not sufficient warmth and elevation of sentiment to deserve the name of a virtuous man. He did not betray or oppress his country; nay, he rendered considerable services to her; but he risked nothing for her. . . . He never put himself prominently before the public eye except at conjunctures when he was almost certain to gain, and could not possibly lose. . . . He avoided the great offices of State with a caution almost pusillanimous. . . . If the circumstances of the country became such that it was impossible to take any part in politics without some danger, he retired to his library and his orchard, and, while the nation groaned under oppression or resounded with tumult and with the din of civil arms, amused himself by writing memoirs and tying up apricots.[38]

Macaulay is not so uncharitable as to believe Burnet's views of Temple's religion, but his conclusion is damning:

He was no profound thinker. He was merely a man of lively parts and quick observation, a man of the world among men of letters, a man of letters among men of the world. Mere scholars were dazzled by the ambassador and cabinet councillor; mere politicians by the essayist and historian. But neither as a writer nor as a statesman can we allot to him any very high place. As a man, he seems to us to have been excessively selfish, but very sober, wary, and farsighted in his selfishness; to have known better than most people what he really wanted in life; and to have pursued what he wanted with much more than ordinary steadiness and sagacity, never suffering himself to be drawn aside either by bad or by good feelings. It was his constitution to dread failure more than he desired success; to prefer security, comfort, repose, leisure, to the turmoil and anxiety which are inseparable from greatness. And this natural languor of mind, when contrasted with the malignant energy of the keen and restless spirits among whom his lot was cast, sometimes appears to resemble the moderation of virtue. But we must own that he seems to sink into littleness and meanness when we compare him, we do not say with any high ideal standard of morality, but with many of those frail men who, aiming at noble ends, but often drawn from the right path by strong passions and strong temptations, have left to posterity a doubtful and checkered fame.[39]

Temple's reputation has never recovered. Macaulay's condemnatory phrases, parroted by H. A. Taine[40] and numerous literary historians, have held forth down to the present. In spite of the lectures by Beaven and Lyttel, as well as the major studies by Marburg and Woodbridge, Temple is still thought of as a bumbling amateur scholar and as an unfortunate diplomat. The twentieth century has forgotten the man who played a minor part in the important events of his time and who wrote some of the most delightful essays of the period between 1660 and 1700.

CHAPTER 10

Epilogue

THE reputation of Sir William Temple has so declined during the more than two and a half centuries since his death that the man has become a footnote in political history and his essays are the long-ignored inhabitants of rare book rooms. Because something in the critical temper will not forgive an error in fact or judgment or shake itself loose from old prejudices, the treatment of Temple and his works at the hands of many critics has been unfair enough to lend credence to Swift's definition of a critic in *A Tale of a Tub: "A Discoverer and Collector of Writers Faults."*

Admittedly, Temple's relevance is not easily discovered because he seems part of an age remote from our own, in which many readers find him either tremendously engaging or disconcertingly alien. The former obligingly overlook any intellectual or scholarly weakness for the sake of Temple's personality or style; the latter, all too often basing their evaluation on the Aesop-Phalaris passages in the essay on ancient and modern learning, proceed to condemn all his other works. As in other areas of judgment, the answer is a more balanced one.

There can be no doubt that Temple himself is certainly one of the more interesting men of the century; he is an excellent example of that combination of the man of action and of contemplation which characterized the seventeenth-century ideal. Deeply involved in some of the great diplomatic adventures of his time, while honestly and doggedly exerting all his powers of logic and persuasion to secure an enduring peace and consequently the well-being of his country, he exercised a keen skill which was ingloriously dulled by a perfidious king and a deceitful ministry. Unsuccessful as his efforts may have been, Temple retained his integrity and honor, and thus rose far above King Charles II and his devious and self-seeking Cabal.

As frustrating as his work among the politicians and intrigues of

Europe may have been, his experiences were rewarding in a less obvious way. He closely observed the manners of those about him and analyzed the cultures of the nations he dealt with, even in their less obvious aspects, such as gardening. From the diplomat evolved the philosopher and historian; the man who could negotiate major treaties and work effectively with the most prominent statesmen of Europe could also write perceptively of the age in which he lived and the nations and cultures which he knew firsthand.

Thus his political experience, as well as his reading and reflection, successfully contributed to his analyses of governments, civilizations, and literatures in which he exhibits an amazingly curious and restless mind, even in his much-maligned essays on learning. Beliefs and customs other than his own—whether they be found among the Dutch, the Chinese, or the Peruvians—stimulated his interest in the distant and exotic. His essays, of course, are of a mixed quality intellectually; at times, he simply did not know enough about the topic at hand or was often uncritical in his acceptance of learned authority. Nevertheless, out of his library, his experience, and his intellectual curiosity he created essays which are still among the best of their kind.

Temple was, however, exclusively neither a politician nor a literary man, as Clara Marburg points out; instead, he must be understood "as an inquiring, impressionable, not very profound mind, trying to find a place for itself in the shifting seventeenth century world of thought" (xviii). Thus, although his work as a diplomat was destroyed by political expediency and his literary reputation marred by a few errors of fact, Temple remains a notable example of the ideal man of the century: a man of talent in public affairs and the arts, one who—like Milton and Dryden and many others—could bring to his writings a life of learning and hard-earned practical wisdom.

That Temple contributed much to the development of the English essay is almost a critical aphorism. In the easy, the dignified, and the rhythmic qualities of his personal essays, we find the first glints of the coming glory in Addison and Steele which was to shine through Goldsmith down to Charles Lamb. Although the influence of Montaigne is evident in some of Temple's work, the Englishman's essays are distinctly his own in the felicity of their style and the gentleness of their spirit.

Temple, however, will always rank with the minor writers in English literature, but as a stylist and an essayist he occupies a notable place. Diplomat, writer, philosopher, historian—these titles will be his as long as the English language survives.

Notes and References

Chapter One

1. *The Works of Sir William Temple, Bart.* (London, 1720), I, 169. All references to Temple's writings, unless otherwise indicated, will be to this edition.
2. Frank Brady, rev. of *Five Miscellaneous Essays by Sir William Temple*, ed. Samuel H. Monk (Ann Arbor, 1963), *Seventeenth-Century News*, XXI (Winter 1963), 68.
3. George Saintsbury, *History of Criticism* (London, 1900–4), III, 401.
4. Swift, *Correspondence*, ed. Harold Williams (Oxford, 1963–65), I, 10; Swift, *Works*, ed. Sir Walter Scott (Edinburgh, 1814), I, xvi.
5. *Early Essays and Romances*, ed. G. C. Moore Smith (Oxford, 1930), p. 5.
6. *Ibid.*, p. 6.
7. *Ibid.*, p. 8.
8. Homer E. Woodbridge, *Sir William Temple: The Man and His Work* (New York and London, 1940), p. 119.
9. *Ibid.*, pp. 216–17.
10. Swift, *Works*, ed. Sir Walter Scott, I, 43.
11. Thomas Babington Macaulay, *The Miscellaneous Works of Lord Macaulay*, ed. Lady Trevelyan (New York, n.d.), II, 549.
12. Clara Marburg, *Sir William Temple: A Seventeenth-Century "Libertin"* (New Haven, 1932), p. xviii.
13. *Ibid.*, pp. 16–18 *passim*.
14. *Early Essays and Romances*, p. 28.

Chapter Two

1. Woodbridge, p. 19.
2. *Ibid.*, pp. 23–24.
3. *The Letters of Dorothy Osborne*, ed. G. C. Moore Smith (Oxford, 1928), p. 21. See also pp. 24, 30, 31, 36.
4. *Ibid.*, p. 42. See also pp. 57, 59, 117, 144.
5. *Ibid.*, p. 81.

6. *Ibid.*, pp. 82, 85, 109.

7. *Ibid.*, pp. 91, 143, 144.

8. *Early Essays and Romances*, p. 36.

9. *Ibid.*

10. *Ibid.*, p. 37.

11. *Ibid.*

12. See *ibid.*, pp. 208–15, for Temple's use of Rosset.

13. *Ibid.*, pp. 208–9.

14. *Ibid.*, p. 81.

15. *Ibid.*, p. 84.

16. *Ibid.*, p. 93.

17. *Ibid.*, p. 113.

18. *Ibid.*, p. xviii.

19. *Ibid.*, p. 35.

20. Woodbridge, p. 28.

21. Thomas P. Courtenay, *Memoirs of the Life, Works, and Correspondence of Sir William Temple, Bart.* (London, 1836), I, 7; II, 338.

22. *Early Essays and Romances*, p. 163.

23. Woodbridge, pp. 24–25.

24. *Early Essays and Romances*, p. 149.

25. *Ibid.*, p. 141.

26. *Ibid.*

27. *Ibid.*, p. 154.

28. *Ibid.*, p. 158.

29. *Ibid.*, p. 146.

30. *Ibid.*, p. 147.

31. *Ibid.*

32. *Ibid.*, p. 157.

33. *Ibid.*, p. 143.

34. *Ibid.*, p. 144.

35. *Ibid.*, pp. 156–66, 170–71.

36. *Ibid.*, p. 165.

37. Woodbridge, p. 25.

Chapter Three

1. For discussions of the climatic theory, which had its origin as early as Aristotle, see Z. S. Fink, "Milton and Theory of Climatic Influence," *Modern Language Quarterly*, II (1941), 67–80, and T. B. Stroup, "Implications of the Climatic Influence in Milton," *Modern Language Quarterly*, IV (1943), 185–89.

2. The social contract had also been assumed by Richard Hooker in *Of the Laws of Ecclesiastical Polity (1594–1597)*. John Locke, the other proponent of the contract, did not advance his theory until

1689, when he published his famous essay *On Civil Government.* Temple, therefore, was probably familiar with the works of Hobbes, Harrington, and Hooker; but he could not have read Locke's essay until after the publication of his own. Even so, Locke did not alter Temple's ideas on the origin of government.

3. The patriarchal concept was not original with Temple. The patriarchal nation is described in the Old Testament Pentateuch, in Plato's *Laws* (Book III), in Aristotle's *Politica*, in Jean Bodin's *La Republique* (1577), and in Sir Robert Filmer's *Observation Concerning the Original of Government* (1652).

4. See my note, "Swift on Standing Armies: A Possible Source," *Notes and Queries*, N.S. X (1963), 215–16.

5. Frank I. Herriott, "Sir William Temple on the Origin and Nature of Government," *Annals of the American Academy of Political and Social Science*, III (1892), 179.

6. [Abel Boyer], *Memoirs of the Life and Negotiations of Sir William Temple* (London, 1714), as quoted in Rae Blanchard, *The Englishman, A Political Journal by Richard Steele* (Oxford, 1955), p. 247.

7. Woodbridge, pp. 126, 128–30.

8. Ellen Douglass Leyburn, "Swift's View of the Dutch," *PMLA*, LXVI (1951), 734–45.

9. *Select Letters to the Prince of Orange* (London, 1701), pp. 204–12 *passim*.

10. *Ibid.*, pp. 213–16 *passim*.

11. This statement is anticipated in his *Observations upon the United Provinces;* see *Works*, I, 60–61.

Chapter Four

1. Swift, *Correspondence*, I, 155–56.

2. Temple's reply to Dunton, written by Thomas Swift from Coddenham, is reprinted in Courtenay, II, 221–23.

3. John Hughes, *Letters by Several Eminent Hands, Including the Correspondence of John Hughes*, ed. John Duncombe (London, 1773), I, 1–10 *passim*.

4. Woodbridge, p. 234.

5. David C. Douglas, *English Scholars* (London, 1939), p. 154.

6. *Ibid.*

7. Woodbridge, pp. 255–57.

8. *Ibid.*, p. 258.

9. *Memoirs of the Life and Negotiation of Sir William Temple* (London, 1714), as quoted in Woodbridge, p. 259.

10. Woodbridge, p. 260.

11. *Ibid.*

12. Douglas, p. 16.

13. Woodbridge, pp. 246–47.

14. *Ibid.*, p. 247.

15. H. V. Routh, "Origins of the Essay," *Modern Language Review,* XV (1920), 146.

16. Woodbridge, pp. 282–90 *passim;* Marburg, pp. 57–68 *passim.*

17. Happy in their Mistake those People whom
   The Northern Pole aspects, whom fear of Death
   (The greatest of all Human Fears) ne'er moves;
   From hence their Courage prone to rush on Steel,
   Their Minds despising Death, they think it mean
   To spare a Life that must again return.
                              (Temple's translation)

18. The so-called Gothic form of government is fully discussed in Samuel Kliger, *The Goths in England: A Study in Seventeenth and Eighteenth Century Thought* (Cambridge, Mass., 1952).

Chapter Five

1. *Early Essays and Romances,* p. 31.

2. The complete prayer is reprinted in Courtenay, II, 373–76.

3. *Ibid.,* 373–74.

4. *Ibid.,* 374.

5. *Ibid.,* 374–76.

6. Marburg, p. 9.

7. Cf. Temple's statement in the essay *Of Popular Discontents* that man possesses "a certain Restlessness of Mind and Thought, which seems universally and inseparably annexed to our very Natures and Constitutions" (*Works,* I, 256).

8. Cf. Swift's estimate of Stoicism in *Thoughts on Various Subjects* (1706): "The Stoical Scheme of supplying our Wants by lopping off our Desires, is like cutting off our Feet when we want Shoes" (Swift, *Prose Writings,* ed. Herbert Davis [Oxford, 1939–63], I, 244).

9. Samuel Johnson used this same definition in 1755. See *Johnson's Dictionary: A Modern Selection,* ed. by E. L. McAdam, Jr. and George Milne (New York, 1963), p. 217.

10. *Early Essays and Romances,* p. 28.

11. As quoted in Woodbridge, p. 232.

12. Thomas F. Mayo, *Epicurus in England, 1650–1725* (College Station, Texas, 1934), pp. 16–17.

13. *Ibid.,* pp. 77–96 *passim.*

14. *Ibid.,* pp. 147–82 *passim.*

15. *Ibid.,* pp. 107–14, 128–43, 185–201 *passim.*

16. The most perceptive and sympathetic treatment of Temple's moral philosophy is in Marburg, pp. 1–25 *passim.*

17. Cf. Swift's satire of similar practices in England in Book IV of *Gulliver's Travels*. (*Prose Writings*, XI, 238).

18. Cf. Gulliver's vivid description of these same remedies (*Prose Writings*, XI, 237–38).

19. Swift, *Prose Writings*, V, 276.

20. *Ibid.*

Chapter Six

1. Samuel H. Monk (ed.). *Five Miscellaneous Essays by Sir William Temple* (Ann Arbor, 1963), p. xxxii.

2. Woodbridge, p. 298.

3. Woodbridge, p. 293n., points out that similar comparisons may be found in Dryden's *Preface to the Fables*, *The Spectator* (nos. 273 and 279), and Pope's *Preface to Homer.*

4. Swift's debt to Temple in *The Battle of the Books* seems obvious; see the episode of the spider and the bee in *A Tale of a Tub*, ed. A. C. Guthkelch and D. Nichol Smith (2nd ed.; Oxford, 1958), pp. 231–32, 234–35.

5. Deborah's song is found in Judges 5:1–31. The reference to a song of Moses is probably to Exodus 15:1–19.

6. According to tradition, Sidney is said to have died at Zutphen in the arms of Sir William Temple (1555–1627), Temple's grandfather. See Woodbridge, pp. 1–2.

7. Cf. the essay *Of Heroic Virtue* (*Works*, I, 215), where Temple credits Odin with the invention of runes.

8. Woodbridge, p. 296.

9. Marburg, p. 92; see also G. M. Miller, *The Historical Point of View in English Literary Criticism* (Heidelberg, 1913), pp. 88–90.

10. Woodbridge, p. 149.

11. *Works*, I, 254.

12. *Early Essays and Romances*, p. 181. Line references are to this edition.

13. Reprinted in *Early Essays and Romances*, pp. 186–89.

14. *Ibid.*, pp. xxvii–xxviii; but see Harold Williams (ed.), *The Poems of Jonathan Swift* (2nd ed.; Oxford, 1958), III, 1068.

Chapter Seven

1. The problems of the ancients-moderns controversy in its wider historical perspective is covered by Hippolyte Rigault, *Histoire de la Querelle des Anciens et des Moderns* (Paris, 1856); Hubert Gillot, *La Querelle des Anciens et des Modernes en France* (Paris, 1914); Anne Burlingame, *The Battle of the Books in Its Historical Setting* (New York, 1920); J. B. Bury, *The Idea of Progress* (London, 1924);

and R. F. Jones, *Ancients and Moderns: A Study of the Rise of the Scientific Movement in Seventeenth-Century England*, 2nd ed. (St. Louis, 1961).

2. Jones, p. 267.

3. Burlingame, p. 159.

4. *Ibid.*, p. 168.

5. *Ibid.*, pp. 120–21.

6. *An Essay Concerning Critical and Curious Learning. By T. R. Esq.* (London, 1698), p. 76.

Chapter Eight

1. Irvin Ehrenpreis, *Swift: The Man, His Works, and the Age* (London, 1962—in progress), I, 102n., believes that Swift first came to Sheen and shortly afterward moved with Temple to Moor Park. See also Woodbridge, p. 219.

2. John Boyle, fifth earl of Orrery, *Remarks on the Life and Writings of Dr. Jonathan Swift* (London, 1752), p. 15; Deane Swift, *An Essay upon the Life, Writings, and Character, of Dr. Jonathan Swift* (London, 1755), pp. 32–33. Denis Johnston, *In Search of Swift* (Dublin, 1959) believes that Swift was actually Temple's half-brother, but his rather sensational theory is effectively exploded by Louis A. Landa in his review of Johnston's book in *Philological Quarterly*, XXXIX (1960), 361–63.

3. Swift, *Correspondence*, I, 1–2.

4. *Ibid.*, 155.

5. Swift, *Poems*, I, 26.

6. Swift, *Prose Works*, ed. Temple Scott (London, 1897–1908), XI, 377.

7. Swift, *Correspondence*, I, 2.

8. *Ibid.*, 10.

9. *Ibid.*, 155.

10. *Ibid.*, 12.

11. Woodbridge, p. 222.

12. Swift, *Correspondence*, I, 12.

13. Swift, *Prose Works*, ed. Temple Scott, XI, 378. Swift was actually twenty-five at this time.

14. *Ibid.*

15. Swift, *Correspondence*, I, 4.

16. *Ibid.*, 12.

17. Louis A. Landa, *Swift and the Church of Ireland* (Oxford, 1954), p. 5.

18. Swift, *Correspondence*, I, 16.

19. *Ibid.*, 17.

20. Swift, *Poems*, I, 52.

21. Swift, *Correspondence*, I, 10. "Lady G." is, of course, Lady Giffard.

22. Swift, *Poems*, I, 49.

23. Landa, pp. 8, 10–15 *passim*.

24. The list is reprinted in Henry Craik, *The Life of Jonathan Swift* (2nd ed.; London, 1894), I, 72; John Forster, *The Life of Jonathan Swift* (London, 1875), p. 100; and *A Tale of a Tub*, ed. Guthkelch and Smith, p. lvi. Unfortunately, there is no extant record of the contents of Temple's obviously well-stocked library.

25. Swift, *Prose Writings*, I, 1.

26. *Ibid.*, 139.

27. Swift, *Works*, ed. Sir Walter Scott, I, 43.

28. *Ibid.*, xvi.

29. The will (dated March 8, 1695) and codicil are printed in Courtenay, II, 484–86.

30. Swift, *Prose Writings*, I, xxxvi.

31. Forster, p. 103.

32. Swift, *Correspondence*, I, 155–56.

33. Julia Longe, *Martha Lady Giffard: Her Life and Correspondence* (London, 1911), p. 246.

34. Swift, *Correspondence*, I, 54.

35. *Ibid.*, V, 6.

36. Swift, *Journal to Stella*, ed. Harold Williams (Oxford, 1948), I, 92; II, 401.

37. *Ibid.*, I, 230–31.

38. *Ibid.*, II, 561.

39. Stephen Gwynn, *The Life and Friendships of Deane Swift* (London, 1935), p. 24.

40. W. D. Taylor, *Jonathan Swift: A Critical Study* (London, 1933), pp. 13–14.

41. See my article, "Swift on Standing Armies: A Possible Source," *Notes and Queries*, N.S. X (1963), 215–16.

42. Robert J. Allen, "Swift's Earliest Political Tract and Sir William Temple's Essays," *Harvard Studies and Notes in Philology and Literature*, XIX (1937), 3–12; Irvin Ehrenpreis, "The Origins of *Gulliver's Travels*," *Publications of the Modern Language Association*, LXXII (1957), 885–98.

43. The possibility that Swift drew upon Temple for his portrait of Lord Munodi is discussed in my article, "Swift's Model for Lord Munodi," *Notes and Queries*, N.S. XII (1965), 216–17.

44. In Temple's essay on learning and Swift's *Battle of the Books*, we find Descartes, Boileau, Paracelsus, and Davenant classified as "moderns"; Aristotle, Galen, and Homer are "ancients."

45. Cf., for example, Temple's comments on modern critics in the

essay on poetry with Swift's in *The Battle of the Books* and *A Tale of a Tub*.

46. For a longer treatment of this possibility, see my article, "Swift and Epicurus," *Bulletin of the Rocky Mountain Modern Language Association*, XVII (1964), 10–12.

Chapter Nine

1. Woodbridge, pp. 334–36.
2. Swift, *Works*, ed. Sir Walter Scott (Edinburgh, 1814), I, 43.
3. Swift, *Prose Writings*, I, 258.
4. *Ibid.*, pp. 270–71.
5. Willard H. Durham (ed.), *Critical Essays of the Eighteenth Century, 1700–1725* (New York: Russell and Russell, 1961), p. 80.
6. *Ibid.*, p. 83.
7. *Ibid.*, p. 79.
8. *Ibid.*, p. 98.
9. *Ibid.*, p. 102.
10. *The British Classics* (London, 1815), XIV, 281–82.
11. Scott Elledge (ed.), *Eighteenth-Century Critical Essays* (Ithaca, New York, 1961), I, 469.
12. *Goldsmith*, ed. George Pierce Baker (New York, n.d.), p. 40. A comparison with Temple's original clearly shows that this borrowing was more than "an unconscious recollection," as Professor Baker would have it; cf. Temple, *Works*, I, 249.
13. Elledge, I, 342, 345.
14. Joseph Spence, *Anecdotes, Observations, and Characters, of Books and Men*, ed. Samuel Weller Singer (2nd ed.; London, 1858), p. 220.
15. *Ibid.*, p. 151.
16. James Boswell, *The Life of Samuel Johnson, LL.D.*, ed. George Birbeck Hill and revised by L. F. Powell (Oxford, 1934), I, 218–19.
17. *Ibid.*, 219, 198n.
18. *Ibid.*, III, 257.
19. Samuel Johnson, *Works* (London, 1820), II, 253.
20. Boswell, II, 234, 421; III, 330; IV, 379.
21. As quoted in Courtenay, II, 261–62.
22. *Ibid.*, 262.
23. Swift, *Prose Writings*, V, 276.
24. Durham, p. 49.
25. *Ibid.*, pp. 49–52.
26. *Ibid.*, p. 55.
27. As quoted in Boswell, III, 257n.
28. David Hume, *The History of England* (New York, 1861), VI, 376.

29. As quoted in Boswell, III, 257n.

30. Charles Lamb, *The Essays of Elia,* ed. Augustine Birrell (London, 1906), p. 233.

31. *Ibid.*

32. Courtenay, II, 252–53.

33. *Ibid.,* 261ff.

34. *Ibid.,* 272.

35. Macaulay, *Miscellaneous Works,* II, 460.

36. *Ibid.,* 461.

37. *Ibid.*

38. *Ibid.,* 461–62.

39. *Ibid.,* 549–50.

40. H. A. Taine, *History of English Literature* (London, 1890), II, 378–83.

Selected Bibliography

PRIMARY SOURCES

1. Books

Observations upon the United Provinces of the Netherlands. London: S. Gellibrand, 1673; Edited by G. N. Clark. Cambridge, England: Cambridge University Press, 1932.

An Essay upon the Advancement of Trade in Ireland. Dublin, 1673.

Miscellanea, the First Part. London: E. Gellibrand, 1679. This volume contains *A Survey of the Constitutions and Interests . . . , Upon the Original and Nature of Government, Upon the Advancement of Trade in Ireland, Upon the Conjuncture of Affairs in October 1673, Upon the Excesses of Grief,* and *Upon the Cure of the Gout by the Moxa.*

Miscellanea, the Second Part. London: R. and R. Simpson, 1690; 1692 ("Corrected and Augmented by the Author"). This second volume of the *Miscellanea* contains *Upon the Gardens of Epicurus, Of Poetry, Of Heroic Virtue,* and *Upon the Ancient and Modern Learning.*

Memoirs of What Past in Christendom, from the War Begun 1672 to the Peace Concluded 1679. London: R. Chiswell, 1691.

Memoirs, the Third Part. From the Peace Concluded 1679 to the Time of the Author's Retirement from Public Business. Edited by Jonathan Swift. London: Benjamin Tooke, 1709.

An Introduction to the History of England. London: R. & R. Simpson, 1695. A revised edition appeared in 1699.

Miscellanea, the Third Part. Edited by Jonathan Swift. London: Benjamin Tooke, 1701. Swift's edition posthumously prints *Of Popular Discontents, Of Health and Long Life, Some Thoughts upon Reviewing the Essay of Ancient and Modern Learning,* and the heads for the essays on life, fortune, and conversation.

Poems by Sir W. T. Privately printed, no date. The only extant copy of this small volume is held by the British Museum.

An Essay upon the Original and Nature of Government. Edited by

Robert C. Steensma. Los Angeles: Augustan Reprint Society (Publication No. 109), 1964.

2. Letters

Letters Written by Sir William Temple and Other Ministers of State. Edited by Jonathan Swift. 2 vols. London: J. Tonson, 1700.

Letters to the King, the Prince of Orange, etc. Vol. III edited by Jonathan Swift. London: J. Tonson, 1703. See Woodbridge, pp. 330–33, for a list of letters not published in either of the above volumes.

3. Collections of Selected Works

Miscellanies. In Four Essays. Glasgow, 1761. Contents: the essays on poetry, ancient and modern learning, gardens, and heroic virtue.

Sir W. Temple's Essays. 2 vols. London: John Sharpe, 1821. Contents: the essays on gardens, health and long life, heroic virtue, poetry, ancient and modern learning, thoughts on reviewing ancient and modern learning, excesses of grief, and the heads on the different conditions of life and fortune, and conversation.

Essays of Sir William Temple. Edited by J. A. Nicklin. London: Blackie and Son, 1903. Contents: the essays on gardens, government, health and long life, poetry, and ancient and modern learning, as well as *Memoirs* Part III.

Upon the Gardens of Epicurus, with Other Seventeenth Century Garden Essays. Edited by A. F. Sieveking. London: Alexander Moring, 1908.

Sir William Temple's Essays on Ancient and Modern Learning and Poetry. Edited by J. E. Spingarn. Oxford: Clarendon Press, 1909.

Early Essays and Romances. With the Life and Character of Sir William Temple by His Sister Lady Giffard. Edited by G. C. Moore Smith. Oxford: Clarendon Press, 1930.

Sir William Temple: Three Essays. Edited by F. J. Fielden. Bombay and Calcutta: Oxford University Press, 1939. Contents: the essays on poetry, popular discontents, health and long life.

Five Miscellaneous Essays by Sir William Temple. Edited by Samuel Holt Monk. Ann Arbor: University of Michigan Press, 1963. Contents: the essays on gardens, heroic virtue, poetry, ancient and modern learning, and thoughts on reviewing ancient and modern learning.

4. Collected Works

The Works of Sir William Temple, Bart. To Which is Prefixed Some Account of the Life and Writings of the Author. 2 vols. London: A. Churchill *et al.,* 1720; Benjamin Motte, 1731. The 1720 edition is the most reliable of the collected editions, but it excludes the romances, the early essays, and some of the poems.

The Works of Sir William Temple, Bart. To Which is Prefixed the Life and Character of the Author, Written by a Particular Friend [Lady Giffard]. 2 vols. London: J. Round, 1740; T. Woodward, 1750; 4 vols. London: J. Clarke, 1757, and J. Brotherton, 1770.

The Works of Sir William Temple, Bart. To Which Is Prefixed the Life and Character of the Author, Considerably Enlarged. 4 vols. London: F. C. and J. Rivington, 1814.

SECONDARY SOURCES

1. Books

BEAVEN, MURRAY L. R. *Sir William Temple.* Oxford: B. H. Blackwell, 1908. Beaven's evaluation of Temple is brief but balanced.

[BOYER, ABEL]. *Memoirs of the Life and Negotiations of Sir William Temple.* London: W. Taylor, 1714. Earliest biography of Temple, concerned mainly with Temple's public life.

COURTENAY, THOMAS P. *Memoirs of the Life, Works, and Correspondence of Sir William Temple, Bart.* 2 vols. London: Longmans, 1836. Courtenay's work is the most complete biography yet written on Temple.

EMERTON, EPHRAIM. *Sir William Temple und die Tripleallianz vom Jahre 1668.* Berlin: Mayer and Muller, 1877. A doctoral thesis at Leipzig and valuable.

[GIFFARD, LADY MARTHA]. *The Life and Character of Sir William Temple, Written by a Particular Friend.* London: Bejamin Motte, 1728. Lady Giffard's sketch is reprinted in Moore Smith's edition of the *Early Essays and Romances* (see above).

HIRSCHBERG, CARL. *William Temples Antheil an der Grundung der Tripleallianz.* Rostock: C. Boldt, 1875. Hirschberg's inaugural dissertation contains little that cannot be found in Woodbridge.

JOHNSTON, DENIS. *In Search of Swift.* Dublin: Hodges Figgis, 1959. Johnston suggests that Temple was Swift's half-brother. For an incisive analysis of this theory, see Louis Landa's review in *Philological Quarterly,* XXXIX (1960), 361–63.

LONGE, JULIA. *Martha Lady Giffard: Her Life and Correspondence.* London: G. Allen, 1911. Sometimes misleading, but contains much information on Temple.

LÜDEN, HEINRICH. *Sir William Temple: Biographie.* Göttingen, 1808. Luden deals mainly with Temple's public career as seen in the memoirs.

LYTTEL, EDWARD S. *Sir William Temple.* Oxford: B. H. Blackwell,

1908. Concerned largely with Temple's political and diplomatic career.

MARBURG, CLARA. *Sir William Temple: A Seventeenth-Century "Libertin."* New Haven: Yale University Press, 1932. Explores Temple's relationship to the intellectual milieu of the late seventeenth century.

WOODBRIDGE, HOMER E. *Sir William Temple: The Man and His Work.* New York and London: Modern Language Association and Oxford University Press, 1940. Frequently confusing in its chronology but this critical biography is the best book on Temple.

2. Articles

ALLEN, ROBERT J. "Swift's Earliest Political Tract and Sir William Temple's Essays," *Harvard Studies and Notes in Philology and Literature*, XIX (1937), 3–12. Swift's *Contests and Dissensions* contains striking parallels to Temple's essays on government and popular discontents.

BENSLY, EDWARD. "The Library at Moor Park," *Notes and Queries*, CLIX (1930), 48. This note briefly summarizes Swift's reading at Moor Park in 1697–98.

BERNARD, F. V. "Swift's Maxim on Populousness: A Possible Source," *Notes and Queries*, N.S. XII (1965), 18. Temple's essays on trade in Ireland and the origin of government may have influenced *A Modest Proposal*.

A. BG. [ANDREW BROWNING]. "Temple, Sir William," *Encyclopedia Britannica*, 1965 ed., XXI, 925–26. A concise account of Temple's private and public life, but ignores his writing.

CASE, ARTHUR E. "Swift and Sir William Temple: A Conjecture," *Modern Language Notes*, LX (1945), 259–65. Case suggests that the initially cool relationship between the two men was the result of Swift's having made "a pig of himself eating green apples" at Sheen in 1687. But there is no reliable evidence that Swift was at Sheen in that year.

CHANG, Y. Z. "A Note on Sharawadgi," *Modern Language Notes*, XLV (1930), 221–24. Temple was probably correct in attributing a Chinese origin to the term.

EHRENPREIS, IRVIN. "The Origins of *Gulliver's Travels*," *Publications of the Modern Language Association*, LXXII (1957), 885–98. Swift's memories of Temple may have provided him with details for his portrait of the King of Brobdingnag.

————. "Swift's History of England," *Journal of English and Germanic Philology*, LI (1952), 177–85. Swift's abstract of English history is based on Temple's *Introduction to the History of England*.

FRENCH, DAVID P. "Swift, Temple, and 'A Digression on Madness,'"

Texas Studies in Language and Literature, V (1963), 42–57. Swift found Temple's Epicureanism intellectually attractive but emotionally repugnant.

HALEWOOD, WILLIAM H. "Young William Temple and Young Jonathan Swift," *College Language Association Journal,* X (1966), 105–13. Swiftian elements are present in young Temple's work.

HANSON, LAURENCE, "Sir William Temple, Pamphleteer," *Times Literary Supplement,* January 15, 1944. p. 36. The *Lettre d'un Marchand de Londres,* mentioned in Arlington's letter of August 24, 1666, may have been written by Temple.

HERRIOTT, FRANK I. "Sir William Temple on the Origin and Nature of Government," *Annals of the American Academy of Political and Social Science,* III (1892), 22–51. Herriott's essay is still the most important discussion of Temple's political theory.

IRWIN, ARCHIBALD B. "Swift as a Translator of the French of Sir William Temple and His Correspondents," *Studies in English Literature, 1500–1900,* VI (1966), 483–98. Evaluates Swift's skill as a translator.

JARRELL, MACKIE. "The Handwriting of the Lilliputians," *Philological Quarterly,* XXXVII (1958), 116–19. Handwriting of the Lilliputians parallels Temple's description of Chinese writing in *Of Heroic Virtue.*

KLIGER, SAMUEL. "Sir William Temple and the Gothic Cult of the Seventeenth Century," *Summaries of Doctoral Dissertations Submitted to the Graduate School of Northwestern University,* X (1943), 25–29. Temple's Gothicism was heavily influenced by sixteenth- and seventeenth-century tradition.

LAMB, CHARLES. "The Genteel Style in Writing." *The Essays of Elia.* Edited by Augustine Birrell. London: J. M. Dent, 1906. Lamb's comments on Temple's essays are both laudatory and enlightening.

LANG, S. and PEVSNER, N. "Sir William Temple and Sharawaggi," *Architectural Forum* (London) CVI (1949), 391–93. Lang and Pevsner summarize various theories of the word's origin.

LEYBURN, ELLEN D. "Swift's View of the Dutch," *Publications of the Modern Language Association,* LXVI (1951), 734–45. Swift's hatred of the Dutch may, in part, have been negatively influenced by Temple.

MACAULAY, THOMAS BABINGTON. "Sir William Temple." *Miscellaneous Works.* Ed. Lady Trevelyan. New York, Harper and Brothers, n.d., II, 459–550. Macaulay's antipathy toward Temple permeates the essay; his assessment of Swift's relationship to Temple is grossly wrong.

MACPHERSON, C. B. "Sir William Temple, Political Scientist?" *Cana-*

dian Journal of Economics and Political Science, IX (1943), 39–54. Temple's writings on political institutions illustrate the use of Baconian methods.

MOORE SMITH, G. C. "Temple and Hammond Families and the Related Families of Nowell and Knollys," *Notes and Queries,* CLI (1926), 237–39. Sir John Temple and his wife were first cousins.

MOORE SMITH, G. C. "Temple and Hammond Families and the Related Family of Harrison," *Notes and Queries,* CLI (1926), 452–53. Discusses other blood relationships among Temple's ancestors.

PIERRE, GERALD J. "Sir William Temple: Friend and Teacher of Jonathan Swift," *Wisconsin Studies in Literature,* No. 2 (1965), 28–36. Points up Temple's influence upon Swift.

ROBBINS, ALICE VIRGINIA. *Sir William Temple's Cabinet, Its History and Why It Failed.* Unpublished master's thesis, University of Chicago, 1902. This thesis treats a topic which has never been fully explored.

ROBERTS, WILLIAM. "Sir William Temple on Orinda: Neglected Publications," *Papers of the Bibliographical Society of America,* LVII (1963), 328–36. Temple's elegy on Katherine Philips may have been his earliest publication (1664?).

ROWEN, HERBERT H. "John de Witt and the Triple Alliance," *Journal of Modern History,* XXVI (1954), 1–14. Believes that Charles II, rather than Temple, was the architect of the Triple Alliance.

STEENSMA, ROBERT C. "The Influence of Sir William Temple on Jonathan Swift: Some Conclusions," *Proceedings of the Utah Academy of Sciences, Arts, and Letters,* XLI (1964), 195–201. Temple's influence is noticeable in Swift's attitudes toward politics, science, and Epicurus.

———. "Swift and Epicurus," *Bulletin of the Rocky Mountain Modern Language Association,* XVII (1964), 10–12. Swift's satire of Epicurus in *A Tale of a Tub* may have been influenced by Temple's essay on gardening.

———. "Swift and Standing Armies: A Possible Source," *Notes and Queries,* N.S. X (1963), 215–16. Swift shared Temple's distrust of standing armies and expressed it in the same metaphor.

———. "Swift's Model for Lord Munodi," *Notes and Queries,* N.S. XII (1965), 216–17. Munodi's character and situation closely resemble those of Temple.

"TEMPLE, SIR WILLIAM," *Dictionary of National Biography.* Ed. Sidney Lee and Leslie Stephen. London: Oxford University Press, 1908–9, XIX, 522–31. The *DNB* article is a factual and fairly accurate account.

"TEMPLE, SIR WILLIAM," *Dictionary of Political Economy.* Ed. R. H. I.

Palgrave (London: Macmillan, 1894–99), III, 528–29. This article briefly treats Temple's economic views.

WEBSTER, C. M. "Temple, Casaubon, and Swift," *Notes and Queries,* CLX (1931), 405. Temple may have influenced Swift to read Casaubon's *Treatise Concerning Enthusiasme* (1655).

Index